To Grandpa Colby and Dad

GRANDPA ED'S BEDTIME STORIES

James E. Martin

James E. Martin

ISBN 0-75961-775-9

This book is printed on acid free paper.

1stBooks-rev. 10/27/05

Table of Contents

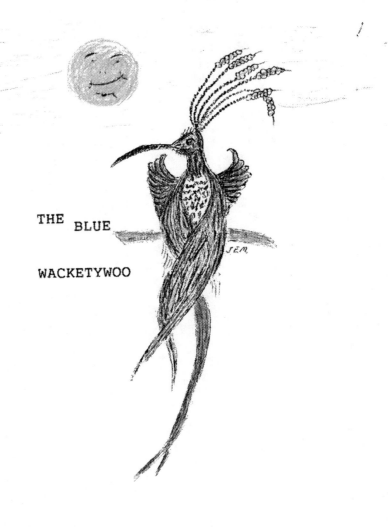

THE BLUE

WACKETYWOO

THE BLUE WACKETYWOO

It has been so long ago since aye first heard this story. Aye was just a wee lad ye know, but times goes so fast, it must have been a hundred years ago. An auld sailor told me that he had visited the world's every port; a salty little auld man who was both narrow and short. An irishman he was with a story mysterious and long. He had a true gift of gab and he said "laddie, aye would tell ye nay wrong."

Aye said to meself, "Just look at him there," his mischevious face beaming with blarney and a snaggled-tooth grin. Beneath great bushy brows, his green eyes twinkled like morning dew on the glen. He was sitting upon a lobster crate near the edge of a pier, carving the image of an elephant from a piece of ivory when aye came near.

He said, "Sit yerself down lad, and aye'll spin ya a yarn. Now this story is true, but as fantastic as ye'll ever larn. It was near Boogalogaland far south of the southern-most south seas, where the jungles are home to giant apes in the trees. Aye was a mere lad, meself, at that very time. Aye hired on a schooner ship as a cabin boy, ye know, jest to keep the captain in line. One night, a fair breeze was blowing, but less than a gale. In the moonlight, the schooner was a beauty to see with its billowing white sails. Across the rolling sea we were racing with the moon who was also racing with the clouds, aye stood alone on bow watch peering across the sea beneath the white shrouds. During the wee hours late at night, water everywhere, no land in sight, the crew was asleep as quiet as could be. Aye felt lonesome like a mere speck amid that vast open sea, when a booming voice came out of the sky. T'was the man in the moon who began talking to me!"

"Ayme needing someone to talk to, am as lonesome as aye can be. Aye have something strange to tell ye, lad, as strange as it may seem, but with me beams of light, aye can see almost everything. I do have many stories that aye could tell you, all strange, but true. Since we are both so lonesome tonight, let me tell one to you. Aye was sailing along," he said, "on a balmy summer night, just like right now on my usual night-time flight over the land of Boogaluga, a spot as fair as can be near where ye are right now south of the southern-most south seas. Aye looked down below, just as aye always do, hoping to see something rare, unusual, and new. And there it was, perched upon a very large limb, a blue

1

wacketywoo regal and prim. Of all of the birds in the world. And there are quite a few, but none are as rare as a blue wacketywoo. They nay can be seen during the day's mid-day light, so iffen ye ere gonna see one, ye gotta see one at night."

Suddenly, the moon's voice became muffled, t'was no longer loud. He was winning the race when he dove behind a very dark cloud. The ocean became ugly as a storm began to brew. The rough waves threatened to break that schooner smack dab in two. The crew awoke, their slumber cut short and the captain began searching for the safety of a port. It was at Boogalugalanld where we found welcomed rest and the crew was set to work mending the rigging which the gale had put to test. Several days would be needed to set things aright, so the best thing that a cabin boy could do was to stay outta sight.

The captain gave me leave the jungle to explore. With a native for a guide, aye was soon making tracks upon the shore. We traveled all day in the jungle's shady light until we could no longer see through the darkness of the night. A small clearing we had reached where we promptly made camp, the darkness dispersed by the light of a kerosene lamp. T'was not long before the moon came up yellow and full. That's when me guide gave me sleeve a terrible hard pull, for with a loud swish and into full view appeared itself, a genuine true blue wacketywoo!

Aye became so excited aye could scarcely contain meself, but aye kept as quiet as a very small elf. That was a once-in-a-lifetime sight aye wanted to see, while the auld 'aye-told-ya-so' moon was a grinning down at me.

Now aye'll do me best to describe to you the plumage and features of a blue wacketywoo. Starting at the top, he had a very long thin curved sharply pointed ice-pick shaped beak and on each side of his head was a broad yellow streak. He had a hacket shaped head at which aye gawked at with awe, topped by six fix foot long plumes tipped by bearded pods like heads of wheat on the end of a straw. His huge round eyes glowed like two hot geen sparks with laser-beam vision to fly in the dark. His fluffy snow white breast looked like the down of a very ripe thistle and he sent shivers through the night with a very weird shrill whistle. Atop his body was a short but gracefully shaped neck, while upon his back was a shield-shaped pacth of light grey specks. Ah! But his wings were so stubby in span, quite miniture and shaped like two upturned Japanese fans! His turquoise blue plumage was thick like very fine velvet covering his body

2

in long flowing whisps like the gracefullly slackened sails of some of the world's tallest ships.

Aye watched in amazement to see what aye see as that marvelous bird picked a kumquat from a kumquat tree. The man in the moon gave me a sly wink.

He boomed, "Aye see ye have found one laddie. Now what do ya think?"

At that very moment a large fluffy white cloud came zooming by, so once more the race was on high in the sky.

"Aye can do that too" said the blue wacketywoo as he crouched for an instant preparing for flight, and with his stubby wings fluttering like those of a humming-bird, he launched into the night.

In only a heartbeat, joined in that lofty race was the blue wacketywoo alongside the moon's yellow face. The white cloud was no match in that wild chase as the moon and the blue wacketywoo sped out of sight into space."

So that story ended for me upon that pier when me father called, "Son, its time that we move on." And with a poof, like magic, the short irishman was gone! Holding me father's hand I looked back as walked along, aye realized that upon that lobster crate had sat a real live leprechaun.

ON THE WAY TO THE ZWIGGLE PIE TREE

BY JAMES E. MARTIN

ON THE WAY TO THE ZWIGGLE PIE TREE

This is a story about a far-away enchanted country called Fliggleland. It has no shoreline, so you can't go there by boat. It is surrounded on all sides by mountains so high they appear to touch the sky, so there are no roads that reach it. Only one passenger at a time can enter or leave Fliggleland. That can only be done by riding in a large wicker basket carried by the claws of a giant eagle.

As a tropical paradise, Fliggleland must certainly be the most beautiful place on Earth. It is a lush green valley where rain never falls and the sun shines brightly every day. The mountainsides are made of white granite cliffs and spires upon which grow graceful dark green pines mixed with beautiful white birch trees. Tall lacy dark green ferns grow between the crags of granite along with thick velvety green moss growing upon the rocks and tree trunks. Hollyhocks, roses, and mountain laurels abound in great profusion throughout the valley floor. Vast meadows are abloom with daisies and sweet clover. Gadzillions of bees and pretty butterflies flit among the flowers. Larks, robins, blue birds, and birds of paradise add to the enchantment of that wonderful place.

Thick glaciers of ice and snow caps the mountain tops. When the warm sun beams upon the snow, it melts and the water tumbles down the mountainsides forming many beautiful lacy waterfalls. The valley's only river carries the crystal clear water to a point where it goes underground into a large cave at the base of a mountain. The little rivlets of water seeping from among the ferns makes a lovely tinkling sound of music which blends with the sighing whisper of the waterfalls.

Fliggleland must be the smallest country in the World. Only a few hundred natives live there. The valley was discoved by an elderly fairy who was forced off course by a violent storm one day as she was being carried in a large wicker basket by her giant eagle. She was amazed when she passed over the high mountains and saw the deep valley bathed in bright sunlight. She had her tired eagle to alight in the valley.

The Fliggleland natives were also amazed at the strange sight of that adult woman riding in a basket carried by an eagle. They formed a crowded ring around the visitors, because those were the only visitors who had ever come to Fliggleland. The friendly natives of Fliggleland were pleased to see the strangers and helped the tired old fairy out of her basket.

Faries as you know, are accustomed to seeing many strange and magic things, because they live in wonderlands. This fairy saw something there in Fliggleland that she had never seen before. All of the people had little arms and legs like Humpty Dumpty, they had no necks, and their bodies were perfectly round and shaped like pies! Every one of them looked exactly alike and the whole front of their bodies were big happy smiling faces. The fairy learned that the reason they looked like pies was because all that they ate was pie. And the reason they were happy was because they ate pies made from the fruit of the Zwiggle Pie Tree. Pies made from Zwiggle fruit is the most yummy best food on Earth. Eat Zwiggle pie and happiness just happens; you just can't help it. It just makes you feel good all over.

The Fligglelanders immediately fell in love with the kindly fairy, so they made her their Queen. Since they had never had a queen before, they also did not have a place for her to live. Well, if you are magic, that was no problem. All the fairy had to do was to wave her magic wand and poof! There stood a lovely little cottage with a thatched roof. The cottage was surrounded by a white picket fence and just oodles and oodles of hollyhocks and roses. In order to travel about the valley and to visit the Zwiggle Tree orchard, all she had to do was make a wave of her magic wand once more to create a pretty little carriage. It had four bright yellow wheels with a pink top whose edge was trimmed with white lace and blue tassels. The carriage was pulled by a team of two large wolly lambs. To complete her household, the fairy queen made room for a fat tabby cat named Wiggle and a little dog named Beagle. Each time the Fairy Queen went for a drive in her carriage, her fat cat rode upon her lap and little Beagle ran alongside barking and wagging his tail.

Oh what a marvelous place was the Zwiggle Pie Tree orchard. There were pie bakeries on both sides of the road a long way before the carriage reached the orchard. The delicious odor of the pies baking inside the ovens could be smelled a mile away upon the warm breeze. Upon arriving at the orchard, the fairy could hardly believe her eyes. The orchard was more like a giant forest of beautiful graceful trees. She had been told that the Zwiggle Pie Fruit was so very good to eat, but she was surprised to see that each piece of the fruit was dark blue and almost as large as a watermelon! What was more, the fruit never stopped getting ripe. Since the sun shined every day, the same trees which bore ripe fruit were also in full bloom. No wonder that the natives of Fliggleland were so happy. The air was filled with the sweetest perfume the fairy had ever smelled.

The happy natives and their children were busy gathering Zwiggle Pie Fruit, which they loaded into two wheeled push carts. Everyone was busy helping eachother. Some worked from ladders leaning against the trees, passing the heavy fruit to those loading the carts, Some pushed the loaded carts to the pie bakeries, while others returned pushing empty carts back to the orchard. All the while, song birds shared the trees with the fruit pickers and filled the air with their beautiful songs. The whole place seemed to be enchanted.

The Fairy Queen realized that Fliggleland would be quickly overcrowded by tourists if the secret of its location was ever discovered. She made up her mind that she would never leave, but she loved little children. She wanted them to share the happiness she had found, so she decided to allow one child per night to visit Fliggleland by riding inside the wicker basket carried by her giant eagle. So, perhaps you can be one of those lucky children to visit that magic place some night. To qualify you must be very young and very small. You MUST MUST MUST believe in fairies and in magic.

If you do, you must lie flat upon your back, cross your ankles, wiggle all of your toes, cross two fingers on each hand, close your eyes, wrinkle your nose, then wiggle and giggle at the exact moment before you fall asleep. Then you must think real hard as you say the magic code: "Fairy Queen from the Land of Fliggle, I've made all of the signs and have wiggled and giggled. Please give me a ride with your giant eagle so I can pet your fat cat named Wiggle, play with your pup called Beagle, and stuff myself with pie made of Zwiggle."

Now you will have to take your chance with many other children who want to go there, too. You must go to bed early in order to get your request in early. Who knows? You may be the next Kid to sit upon the carriage seat beside the Fairy Queen as the two wolly lambs make the journey to the Zwiggle Pie Orchard. You see, I am much too old to get an invitation to visit Fliggleland. If you ever get to go, please write to me about your trip. Address your letter to: Grandpa Ed, Department of Bedtime Stories, HC 30, Box 183, Caldwell, WV 24925

Pleasant dreams,
Your old Friend
Grandpa Ed

GRANDPA ED'S BEDTIME STORIES

THE STORY OF
THE DOGHOUSE MOUSE

BY JAMES E. MARTIN

THE STORY OF THE DOG HOUSE MOUSE

Mrs. Mouse lived inside a very large city. Being a mouse, she was quite small and dainty. Her Mother had taught her to always be quiet, polite, and refined. Life in a large city was very dangerous for small animals such as Mrs. Mouse when they went shopping for food. In addition to crowds of people with their big feet which could crush a little mouse, there were prowling dogs and cats, speeding cars, trucks, motorcycles, and people riding roller blades to watch out for. Another thing that made Mrs. Mouse nervous was the endless noise. Honestly, it never ceased. It seemed to grow louder with every passing day. The horns, the screeching tires, the clatter of the commuter trains, the jet planes and helicopters; it became almost impossible to sleep. All of that stress was causing Mrs. Mouse's dainty little nose to develop a nervous twitch. There came a day when she could endure those conditions no longer. That was when she decided to move to the suburbs. She packed her few belongings, told her friends good-bye, and began the journey away from the city.

Mrs. Mouse had never traveled outside the city before, so she did not know exactly where she was going. She had to plan very carefully for her personal safety during the trip. She knew that, although she, herself, was refined and considerate of others, mice have almost no friends among other creatures on earth. Some mice whom she had known met with terrible accidents either from encounters with humans, being caught in traps, ran over by cars, and by some other creatures who think of mice as their dinner. She knew that every step of her trip to the suburbs could be filled with danger. If she planned to travel by day, she would have to select a route where she would be hidden from view beneath thick grass or under growing shrubbery. She would have to move only a few feet at a time, pause to observe the area around her, watch for danger, and then move on. She would always have to search ahead for a place to take shelter if danger appeared. Except in dire emergency, she would have to move slowly so as not to attract attention, because there was always the chance she may encounter a large snake or be pounced upon from above by a hawk. She would rather have traveled at night, but there could even be more dangers during darkness. Night time is when hungry cats prowl with their sharp eyes and keen senses of smell. Mice are also the favorite

9

food of owls who perch in trees and have eyes that can see through the darkness like laser beams. What is even more scary, owls not only fly swiftly, they make absolutely no noise when they fly. A mouse on the ground has no warning that an owl is about to strike. Mrs. Mouse decided to travel only during daylight, mostly during the mid-day when the sun was hot and cats, hawks, and snakes are less active.

Because she had to be so cautious, Mrs. Mouse did not travel very far each day, but eventually she reached the outer limits of the city and began seeing the more open spaces of the suburbs. One thing which improved her safety and also speeded her progress where lawn fences under which she could travel quickly and out of sight. Adding to that new advantage were lush flower beds and a great variety of dense shrubbery which hid her from view.

It was in this strange new world that Mrs. Mouse began to see beautiful houses sitting in the midst of lush green lawns. That was, however, when she discovered a dreadful new danger. She was hiding in a flower bed at the end of a lawn when she saw two men using some kind of very noisy contraptions.

She had seen many men before, but what were those things they were using? She crept behind a fence post and remained motionless as one of the men passed close to her pushing a gasoline powered lawn mower. She was fighting the urge to flee in panic when she was caught by total surprise as the second man followed close behind the first trimming the edge of the lawn with a weed eater. It was snipping off the grass only a few inches from where Mrs. Mouse was hiding. Her legs were so weak from fright that she could not run even if she tried and her poor nervous nose was almost twitching off her face!

After the two men passed her position, she gathered her strength to scamper under the fence in the opposite direction. She ran to the corner and then followed the fence to the back lawn and continued across the next property behind that house. Anything which would put distance between herself and those awful noise machines. That was when she discovered a large dog house. As she approached the dog house, she spied a crack in its foundation which was wide enough for her small body to squeeze through. She rushed into the dark safety of the dog house to hide while she calmed her nerves. From her new-found refuge, the sound of the lawn machinery in the neighboring lawn was now only a distant purr. "Whew!" she said. "That monster nearly scared me to death!"

It was not long before her eyes became accustomed to the darkness. To her delight, she discovered that the dog house had a double floor. The space she was in was neat and snug. What was more, it looked like a safe place to be. Mrs. Mouse was much too considerate of others to make her home in a place that belonged to someone else, but considering the fact that the space was empty and could be entered only through a narrow crack, she was almost certain that no one else owned it. She really wanted this to be her new home. It was the kind of place she had often dreamed about. For the first time in her life, she could have a clean spacious place to live where nobody would bother her. She would gather some of the loose grass that the lawn mower was leaving behind to make herself a warm comfortable nest. There would be plenty of space for storing food and she discovered that her upstairs neighbor in the dog house was a very large ugly bench-legged bull dog whose only interests in life were eating and sleeping. Mrs. Mouse only looked at the dog from a safe distance, but after living in her new home for a few days, she learned that the dog had absolutely no interest in her. He showed no hostility. He was so lazy that he would not even lift his head off the floor of the dog house when she would stare at him. He would merely open one of his terrible red rimmed eyes and look blankly back at her. There was one thing certain, Mrs. Mouse would not have to fear any harm from cats or snakes with Old Bull Dog, her personal security system, guarding her home.

How fortunate could one mouse be? Mrs. Mouse had a wonderful new home, but also, what a beautiful place it was with the owners living in a lovely cottage surrounded by a white picket fence. Shrubbery and great beds of flowers grew throughout the velvety green lawn. Wonders of all

11

wonders! The owners also grew a vegetable garden where Mrs. Mouse could find an endless supply of food and dried seeds to store away for winter. In addition to all of that, Old Bull Dog did not mind sharing the food he spilled over the side when he thrust his short blunt snout into his dish. The owners installed bird feeders during the winter months and Mrs. Mouse could creep out at night and find a wide choice of tasty seeds to eat. Mrs. Mouse was absolutely certain that no matter how far she traveled or how widely she searched, she could not have found a better place to live than this one she accidentally stumbled upon. She was sure that she had found The Garden of Eden and only two members of that wonderful place knew that she was there – just Mrs. Mouse and Old Bull Dog. She was sure that her upstairs neighbor would never tell. Memories of the hectic city life almost faded from memory with the passing of time. Mrs. Mouse lived happily ever after.

Have happy country bed time dreams,
"Grandpa Ed"

GRANDPA ED'S BEDTIME STORIES

DADDY! THERE'S A SKUNK IN MY BUNK!

BY JAMES E. MARTIN

James E. Martin

THERE IS A SKUNK IN MY BUNK

Little Tommy was ready for bed. He had taken a nice warm bath, he had brushed his teeth, and he was wearing his pajamas. He had put his wooly little terrier named Mop to bed, so now he was ready to crawl into his own bunk bed and go to sleep. But first, he wanted his Mommy to read him a bedtime story.

He called to his Mommy, "I'm ready for bed Mommy. Will you please tuck me in and read me a story?"

"Why, of course, Tommy. I will be happy to," she replied as she came into his room and sat on the edge of his bed.

Tommy's favorite stories were those about animals, especially those who lived in the forest. The one that his Mommy read to him that night was about Perfuma Skunk. The setting for the story was during the fall of the year when the leaves were coming down and the cold winds were beginning to blow. It was also the time of the year when pods of grapes were ripe and the nuts and acorns were falling to the ground. Animals such as squirrels, ground hogs, raccoons, possums, bears, beavers, foxes, minks, weasels, and otters were busy preparing their dens for winter. Some worked hard every day storing food to eat when the deep snow came. Many of the animals who sleep all winter were busy lining their beds with warm dry leaves.

Little Perfuma Skunk had not had a very happy life. Her mother and father had met with a terrible accident while robbing a farmer's chicken house one night when she was quite young. She was left without any family to take care of her. She was a very pretty little animal with a cute little pointed nose, sparkling black eyes, little round ears, and four dainty little feet. And ah! Her coat! It was such a beautiful coat. It was a glossy black with two broad snow white stripes which extended from the back of her head all the way to the very tip of her fluffy long tail. She was the fanciest animal in the entire forest.

Perfuma had one great problem, however. By not having a Mommy to teach her about the importance of hygiene, Perfuma never took a bath. She was friendly and gentle. She had very nice manners. She was not mean and spiteful. She was a perfect lady in every way, but she smelled so badly that the other animals would not stay near her. Her odor became so bad that the other animals began calling her 'Little Stinker.' It became

14

so glad that, if Perfuma came into another animals's home for a visit, they would leave their den and not return. Sometimes when a family of other animals would return home after a hike in the forest, they would find Perfuma Skunk waiting for them inside their den. The youngsters, who would always race ahead of their slower parents, would rush into their home, but would dash back outside shouting with alarm, "There is a skunk in our bed!"

Poor Perfuma. What was she to do? No one wanted to be her friend. She did not know anything about making dens, besides she was not yet old enough to have seen a winter. It was certain that her neighbors did not care if she lived or died. They just wanted her to stay as far away from them as possible. That was just what Perfuma decided to do. She would go far far away.

One day, nearly exhausted, Perfuma came upon an old abandoned farm. All of the buildings were rundown and sagging. There was a barn made of logs which she explored. Much to her delight, large heaps of hay lay inside the barn. Perfuma tunneled into the hay and made herself a warm dry den. Inside her new den, the winter wind and snow could never reach her. Also much to her delight, she discovered that some human had used the garden plot behind the barn to grow vegetables, a surplus of which remained unharvested. Perfuma had been starving hungry for days, but now she had so much food she hardly knew what to do with all of it. But Perfuma was not dumb. She had seen the other animals storing food for winter. Having been hungry for so long and, having felt the chill in the air, she now understood why the other animals were making their dens warm and comfortable. Perfuma prepared a large storage area beneath the hay where she stored a large supply of tasty vegetables from the garden.

One day after much hard work, Perfuma returned to her den and right there before her eyes was another skunk lounging in her bed.

"Hi!" said the stranger. "My name is Fragrant Skunk. I hope that I did not startle you. You see, I have been searching for a place to live and needed a place to rest. I discovered your comfortable home and decided to wait for you to return. I could tell by the smell that another skunk lived here."

"Startled? Yes, but I am wonderfully glad to welcome you," replied Perfuma. "You see, I am all alone since my parents died and I have no friends. It is so good to see you. I hope that you will stay and share my home with me."

James E. Martin

So the story that Tommy's Mommy was reading to him ended with, "together Perfuma and Fragrant Skunk lived happily ever after.

Tommy's Mommy looked at her little son as his eyelids drooped as he was falling asleep. She kissed him goodnight as he murmured, "I love you Mommy."

His Mommy turned out the light and left the room. Unnoticed and very quiet, someone else had been listening to Mommy's story.

Little Mop, the terrier, had heard the cold wind howling outside the house. Oh sure, his dog bed was warm and comfortable, but that howling wind disturbed him. He did not like the way it sounded, so he wanted to go some place where he could not hear it. Besides, he liked to be as close to his good friend Tommy as he could get, so he quietly crept under Tommy's bunk while Mommy was reading the story.

Mop remained motionless for awhile after Mommy turned out the light. He knew that Tommy would not mind if he spent the night in his bunk, but he wanted to be certain that Tommy was sound asleep before he made his move. He climbed atop Tommy's bunk and found an opening between the covers and Tommy's back, then he burrowed his way under the covers all the way to Tommy's feet.

While Tommy's Mommy and Daddy were watching a late show on television, Tommy was dreaming about furry woods animals who were scurrying about among the dry leaves hunting nuts and making their dens. He also dreamed about Perfuma Skunk crawling into someone else's bed. Somehow he imagined that he had gotten into his own bed and found her waiting there. He stirred slightly in his sleep when his foot touched Mop's furry body. Tommy let out a scream so loud that he could be heard all the way to Cincinnati!

16

"Daddy! There is a skunk in my bunk!" he shouted as he raced out of his room.

His parents rushed into his room and turned on the light.

"Where? Where?" they shouted.

"There at the foot of my bed," exclaimed Tommy.

Tommy's Daddy yanked the covers off the bunk and there he was, a very sheepish looking little terrier named Mop.

Have happy country bed time dreams,

"Grandpa Ed"

GRANDPA ED'S BEDTIME STORIES

PERKINS

BY JAMES E. MARTIN

18

PERKINS

Mother Cat certainly had her paws full each day trying to keep her home neat and tidy, searching for food for her family, mending cat suits, and knitting mittens for her kittens during cold winter weather. Mother Cat was a very kind and loving old tabby cat. She was well known and respected throughout the community. Her husband, McGreggor Cat, was also well known as a cat-about-town. His interests often kept him away from home several days and nights each month, making it necessary for Mother Cat to manage the children and the family home by herself. That was much the same pattern among most of the neighborhood cat families whom she knew. Although Mother Cat's two children were very nice, they were also young, healthy, and very rambunctious. When they became playful, which actually was most of the time, her daughter, Mitty Kitty, and her son, Perkins, could really make a mess of the house.

Mother Cat tried to be understanding, remembering how mischievous she, herself, had been when she was a kitten. Her two kittens could really try her patience though, as was the time when they both had climbed up a tree and could not get down. The fire department had to be called to rescue them. That was bad enough, but the kittens enjoyed seeing the fire trucks so much, they climbed back up the tree a few more times so that they needed rescued again. A wise old fireman realized what was happening so he gave mother cat a warning that if it happened again, the kittens would be arrested and taken to the animal pound to be punished. Following that, she 'grounded' the kittens inside the house for a week, but they caused so much trouble they nearly drove her crazy. Once they removed a very expensive roll of yarn from Mother Cat's knitting basket. That yarn was of a special color from which Mother Cat planned to make herself a beautiful sweater. The kittens became so hopelessly entangled that they could not even more their legs. Mother Cat was in the kitchen preparing a meal of porrage, mouse pot-pie, and catnip tea. When she heard their terrible cries for help, she almost had a heart attack. The more the kittens tried to free themselves, the worse they became entangled. In the end, Mother Cat had to cut the yarn into many pieces just to free them. She was really disgusted with the kittens, because, earlier during the day, they were roughhousing all over the furniture when they knocked a large pot of geraniums off a table and spilled potting soil on Mother Cat's clean carpet. As though that wasn't enough, they caused Mother Cat great distress when one of them knocked Mother Cat's prized picture of her parents, Effie and Mortimer Cat, off an end table and shattered the glass. She cried for two hours following that. Oh! If only her husband, McGreggor Cat could be home more often to help raise those two pesky kittens! Where was he when she really needed him?

As time went by, Mitty and Perkins grew into two handsome adult cats. Mitty was very much like her mother with silky long black fur that rippled in the breeze. She had beautiful long eyelashes and had a large fluffy tail with a white tip. The color of her throat, breast, and stomach was snow white and she had four white stocking feet. Her eyes were dark green and her purr was as quiet as a distant water fall. Her manners were most ladylike and she never meowed in a loud voice.

Handsome Perkins, on the other hand, was huge and rowdy. Like his father, his fur was marked by black tiger stripes on grey. He began spending much of his time with his father and several of the other young tomcats in the neighborhood. Mother Cat worried that Perkins would get in with the wrong crowd, but Perkins' father just said not to worry, that toms will be toms; what could he possibly do that would cause any harm?

Just like his father, Perkins began staying out late at night, then wanted to lay about the house to sleep all day. Sometimes, he stayed out all night walking fences, raiding trash cans, caterwauling at the moon, and disturbing people's sleep. He and his friends especially enjoyed tormenting dogs who responded by baking loudly causing many bad tempers within the community. Perkins expected his mother to prepare his meals, but would do nothing to help clean up the messes he made about the house. His poor mother was deeply disappointed by the way he was acting.

One day, Mother Cat's sister Nellie and her husband McDuff Cat arrived on a visit from Boston. McDuff was very successful in business and had amassed a fortune in mouse futures and cat food in the stock market. He was a gruff no-nonsense old cat who belonged to the finest country clubs, wore plaid checkered smoker jackets, and smoked a big briar pipe with a crooked stem which caused the bowl to lay upon his chest. Although he wasn't crippled, he carried a fancy walking cane with an expensive gold knob which was shaped to resemble a rat's head. McDuff had a very low opinion of McGreggor, his brother-in-law, whom he regarded as a lazy loafer. He had an even greater dislike for his brash young nephew, Perkins, whom he said would never amount to a pile of cat treats.

McDuff did not want to pay that visit, but his wife, known to the family as 'Nervous Nellie' insisted that she wanted to visit her only sister. McDuff, who could not stand to be around gossiping females and who refused McGreggor's invitation to spend a few evenings with him and some of his rowdy friends engaging in cat fights, taunting dogs, and keeping people awake, just contented himself by visiting the local tobacco store and news stand where he bought the daily copy of the Cat Street Journal. He settled himself into a comfortable chair in Mother Cat's living room where he spent the time reading and smoking his pipe.

Perkins had a great dislike for his aunt and uncle. He wished that he could do something to make them go back home as soon as possible. For one thing, each time they came to visit, Nervous Nellie would cause Mother Cat to cry because of Nellie's continuous tongue lashing about how Mother Cat had nothing of value, McGreggor Cat was a worthless bum, and how she was allowing Perkins to grow up to be just like his father. Perkins knew that Aunt Nellie kept herself in such a frenzy that she had to constantly take bicarbonate pills to settle her nervous stomach. Her nerves were so jangled that she could not got to sleep at night without sedating herself with huge doses of catnip. Sometimes she could not go to sleep until one or two o'clock after midnight.

Perkins and some of the other young toms began making plans as how to send his aunt and uncle packing. McDuff, who could sleep like the dead, would never sleep in the same room with Nervous Nellie because of her constant tossing and turning. For that reason, Mother Cat allowed Aunt Nellie to sleep alone in one of the guest rooms on the second floor; McDuff used another room just down the hall.

It was Halloween Night and many of the neighborhood cats were out to celebrate cats best holiday of the year. They were visiting old abandoned houses, squalling, hissing, fluffing up their fur, and arching their backs – all of the usual things that cats do on Halloween Night. Of course, Mother Cat and her visitors were much too refined to take part in anything so undignified as that, so did not take part in the celebration. Perkins and his friends were having the time of their lives when Perkins had a great idea. Why not liven things up around his house? Why not give his stuffy relatives a night to remember? He told his pals his idea. They thought it would be 'a blast', so a dozen of the young toms went pussy footing over to Perkins' house.

The weather was warm, the moon was full and bright. Perkins' home had no air conditioning, so it was easy to see that Aunt Nellie's bedroom window was open for ventilation. A rose trellis was attached to the outside wall of the house and it extended from the ground right up to the sill of Aunt Nellie's window. Perkins had climbed the trellis many times when he did not want Mother Cat to know how late he was staying out. Now he climbed the rose trellis as his friends watched from below. Perkins climbed ever so quietly until he was standing atop the windowsill. He could see Aunt Nellie's body lying in the bed in the moonlight. As quick as lightning, Perkins launched himself inside the room with a powerful leap at the same time emitting a most dreadful hiss and loud squall as he landed on top of Nervous Nellie with all four feet!

The old cat let out a screech of terror, exploded out of that bed, flung open the bedroom door, and went racing down the hall as though all of the demons on earth were following her. Needless to say, no one in that house had any more sleep that night. Nervous Nellie was beside herself and could not be calmed. She looked ridiculous when the others searched the room to find the terrible intruder whom she said had terrorized her, but no one could be found. Nellie insisted that she and McDuff begin packing immediately to return home, because she refused to spend another night, not another minute in that terrible house. They were on their way to the depot before daybreak. They even refused to eat breakfast.

Shortly after they departed, a very innocently acting Perkins arrived home for breakfast. Mitty Kitty had suspicion that what had happened to Aunt Nellie was not just her imagination. She glanced over the breakfast table at Perkins with a sort of inquisitive look.

She asked, "Did you have an exciting Halloween Night, Perkins?"

"Meow", he murmured as he gave Mitty Kitty a sly wink.

With oodles and bedtime love,
"Grandpa Ed"

James E. Martin

GRANDPA ED'S BEDTIME STORIES

BUTTONS

24

BUTTONS

This story begins with a lonely little teddy bear named Buttons who lay inside a toy box that was as dark as a dungeon. The toy box was stored at the back of a closet under a pile of shoes and garmets. Once there was a darling little girl who awakened one Christmas morning and saw for the first time the same little bear sitting where Santa Clause had placed it under her Christmas tree. He had a pleasing smile on his face, his beady little black eyes gleamed brightly in the tree lights, he wore a plaid bow-tie, and a little bright red jacket with two large white buttons on the front. The tiny girl squealed with joy as she dashed across the room and gathered the bear into her arms, pressed him to her breast with a hug, and shouted.

"Oh buttons! I hoped so much that you would be waiting for me. Oh Buttons! Buttons! I love you!"

From that moment onward for seven years, Buttons and that little girl spent many happy hours every day as the very closest of friends. Buttons was always an important guest when the little girl had her little girlfriends over to her house for tea parties and games. Buttons often rode inside doll carriages, was pushed in swings, and rode slicky-slides. Everyone seemed to love Buttons. When it became bed-time and the little girl's Mommy tucked her into bed, Buttons was always cuddled by the little girl's loving arms. Buttons went everywhere the little girl went, even on vacation trips with her family or when she went to visit Grandma.

Buttons was a very happy little bear. Surely no other little bear could be as fortunate as he, but little by little as time went by, Buttons began seeing his sweet friend less and less. As the little girl grew older, she had fewer tea parties, she no longer took Buttons for rides in her doll carriage, and she and her friends had pajama parties to which Buttons was not invited. He was now spending most of his time sitting upon a shelf in the little girl's bedroom. The girl had different interests now. She was learning to play the flute in school, she became a crossing guard on a street corner near her school, and she became a member of a girl's softball team. She was much too busy to spend any time with Buttons. Late one summer evening, the little girl who was rapidly becoming a big girl, came dashing into her bedroom following a championship ball game. She glanced about her room looking for a place to display her newly won championship trophy.

"Ah ha!", she said. "This is a perfect place" as she swooped Buttons from his place upon the shelf, placed the bright new trophy on the spot where he had been, and tossed him headfirst into that old toy box where he joined many other long-forgotten toys. What was even worse, the toy box also became the target for smelly old sneakers, gym socks, and dusty ball gloves.

Years passed. The girl graduated from high school and went away to college. One day the girl's Mother opened the closet door and said, "Whew! Those old socks and sneakers smell bad! I'll clean them and give them to someone who can use them."

With that, she closed the lid of the toy box and closed the closet door. Buttons ached for someone to cuddle him, but he just went unnoticed lying there inside the dark old box. Nobody ever came to visit him, so he just grieved away the long boring years.

From inside the box, Buttons could often hear voices of people inside the house and he would remember those happy days before he was forgotten. One day he heard the girl's Mother come rushing into the bedroom. She and another lady were talking excitedly about a wedding. They were hustling about cleaning and dusting. The vacuum cleaner was whirring. They even cleaned and dusted inside the closet. Clothing was rearranged and most of the little girl clothing was packed into boxes and moved to the attic.

Buttons could not see the activity from the dark box, but he was wondering who was going to be married. In a few days, his question was answered. The wedding was for his old friend! He could hear all of the people's excited voices and at last she arrived inside her bedroom! Her voice was different now, but it was so very beautiful. She and her Mother chatted excitedly as her Mother helped her dress for her wedding.

At long last her Mother said, "Alright Darling. You are ready. Your Father will be knocking on your door in a few minutes. He will walk down stairs with you just as soon as the music starts."

She kissed her daughter and closed the door.

Buttons wished so much that he had a voice. He tried to shout "Please! Please! Please hear me. I'm here!" Suddenly there was a knock upon the bedroom door and a piano began playing 'Here comes the Bride.'

Buttons was sure that his heart would break as he heard the bedroom door quietly close. The next time that he heard the door open was late that night after the reception. Buttons heard a strange male voice as the girl and her new husband returned to the room to gather her luggage before leaving for their honeymoon.

"I have never loved anyone and anything as much as I love you," the girl said as the two lovers embraced. Buttons heard their footsteps upon the stairs as they departed. He had never felt so sad and alone.

Months of long days and nights came and passed as Buttons lay in his lonely prison. He yearned just to hear a child's voice or children's happy laughter. He wonder if there was such a person as a fairy god-mother who could rescue poor forgotten teddy bears, but a fairy god-mother never came. Also silently waiting were all of the little girl's dolls and other toys, but none of them understood bear talk. What was he to do?

After what seemed forever, there came a day when once more Buttons heard another great stir of excitement as the girl's Mother and some other women burst into the bedroom. He could hear them raise the windows and pull back the curtains. The women began cleaning, dusting, and rearranging furniture. Of course, Buttons could not see what they were doing, but it seemed that they were moving something new into the room. He sensed that something wonderful was going to happen. Then late one afternoon, Buttons heard the doorbell ring. Someone was arriving and there was much hugging, laughing, and excited talking. That is when it happened! Buttons heard the sound of a baby cooing. He became so excited that he almost jumped out of the box! Soon there were many voices as neighbors joined the happy grandparents. Everyone was ooing and ahing over the little baby. After a while, the Grandmother said to her Daughter,

"Come up to your old bedroom. We have made it into a nursery." Soon there were many voices inside the room and the baby was happily cooing.

Button's old friend said, "We are so disturbed. The airline lost all of our luggage. The baby's only clothing for now is what I have in this shoulder bag and her only toy is this little rattle. I hope she can make do with that until they find our things.

"Why Mary Ann", her Mother said. "Have you forgotten Buttons? He is right here in your old toy box, right where you left him!"

Before Buttons had time to move a whisker, Mary Ann's Mother yanked the lid open on that dark box. The bright light nearly blinded Buttons. He suddenly felt himself being hoisted into the air and his heart burst with joy as once more he saw his beloved Mary Ann and she crushed him to her breast.

All of the happy memories came rushing back as she sobbed, "Oh my darling Buttons! How could I ever stop loving you? Look, I have brought you another playmate!"

With that, she placed Buttons into the curl of Baby Cindy's chubby little arm. Baby Cindy said, "Cooo-o-o-o" as she nuzzled Button's cheek with a drooling little kiss. Buttons knew the meaning of "Cooo-o-o-o", which in baby talk means "Buttons, I wooove you." Of course you knew that already.

You be sure to have happy dreams.
With Country Love,
"Grandpa Ed"

GRANDPA ED'S BEDTIME STORIES

POPPY'S HAT SHOP

BY JAMES E. MARTIN

James E. Martin

POPPY'S HAT SHOP

It was easy to tell that Poppy was a happy little girl. She laughed a lot and had a bright little smile. She was also happy because she had a mother and father who loved her. What was more, she had a best friend named Sally. Poppy's mother and Sally's mother were partners in a women's apparel shop in a small town located in warm sunny Florida.

The two mothers wanted to spend every day with their daughters, so they took Poppy and Sally to work with them. To make certain that their daughters were content, their mothers prepared a playhouse inside one small room of their shop where the two children could do whatever they wanted. One nice thing about the playroom was that it had a back door which opened onto a fenced-in back lawn with shade trees. The back lawn was safe from wandering dogs and strangers. It was a place where the girls could run and exercise. The mothers had workers to install swings, a sandbox, a teeter totter, slicky slide, and a wading pool. They also built a picnic table.

Inside the playroom, the mothers installed a small sales counter, a toy cash register, telephone, and sewing machine so that the girls could play like they owned their own apparel shop. There were clothes racks, coat hangers, and lots of dresses, hats, and shoes which the girls had outgrown. In addition to that, the mothers provided them with frilly handkerchiefs, scarves, gloves, some brightly colored umbrellas, and some purses. So that they could design their own costumes, their mothers provided the girls with scraps of cloth saved from alterations which they could use to cut with blunt tipped scissors and sew with needle and thread. Oh! What a wonderful shop!

Poppy dearly loved hats of all kinds. Over time, she gathered broad brimmed hats, hats with brims turned up in front with a large flower on it, tam-o'-shanter hats, rain hats, hats trimmed with artificial fruit, floppy hats, hats with feathers, hats with veils, hats with ribbons, straw hats, felt hats, domed hats, flat hats, witch hats, pirate hats, even a Dr. Seuess 'cat-in-a-hat' hat.

Ah! the fun those girls had. When the mother's customers brought over little girls shopping in the adult apparel shop, Poppy and Sally would invite them to visit their shop too. They imagined that they had fantastic sales where stylish women would come to buy. They also held gala lawn parties where stylish women would dance and dine upon tea and tarts. The girls would clothe themselves in fancy dresses, high heeled shoes, white gloves, large plumy hats, dangling purses, frilly shawls, and pretty parasols. They would pretend that they were famous models stepping daintily along a runway before crowds of cheering admirers.

Once in awhile, they would create bright water colored posters announcing a great imaginary sale. They would dress themselves in fancy clothing, then stand before a large glass mirror holding their posters pretending that they were looking at themselves on television as they modeled their merchandise.

It is important that girls giggle a lot. You see, if girls are not giggling, it is hard to tell if they are having fun or not. To make sure that there was no shortage of giggles, sometimes Poppy would create very silly ads for her television show. There were times when she wrote little rhymes about the things which they had for sale. The more silly the ad, the more the girls giggled. One ad announced:

This is Poppy from Poppy's hats
We have a Poppy's hat for you
If you like your Poppy's hat
You may want more than one or two
You will look just swell in a Poppy's hat
Be you thin or very fat
You will look great. I promise that
In your extra special Poppy's hat

Now we have hats for animals, too
Names starting with A to K for kangaroo
Or L for leopards and monkeys, too
To Z for all other animals in the zoo
We have hats for all kinds of cats
Big ones for elephants, small ones for bats
Tall ones for giraffes, wee ones for gnats
Straw hats for goats and cheese ones for rats

We have every kind of hat for dogs
For chickens and turkeys, pigs and hogs

31

And for chubby old beavers who live in the bogs
We even have rain hats for very green frogs
We have hats in our attic for polar bears
For snowshoe rabbits and marsh hares
Hats for squirrels or baby whales
Or sly red foxes with fancy tails

We have hats for vultures and woodpeckers, too
Mining hats for ground moles
Sometimes called a shrew
Hats for bobbin robins and all birds that sing
We have hats for almost anything
We have many hats with peculiar shape
We can even fit a sun bonnet upon an ape
A football helmet on a rhinoserous
Or a jockey hat upon a hippopotomous

Our firemen's hat will make hyenas laugh with glee
And a sombrero on a turtle is funny to see
But the strangest of all to us
Is to see a cowboy hat upon a duck billed platypus
We have down filled hats fit for a goose
Hats with horn holes to be worn by a moose
Hats that a snake can crawl into to sleep
And wooly knit hats to be worn by a sheep

We have some hats that can be worn in the house
Fit for a spider, a cricket, or even a mouse
Hats for gophers digging holes in the golf course
Hats for French poodles or even a horse
We have hats for wearing to school
Or crazy hats for the day of April Fool
To wear to church or when hanging upside down from a limb.
Or to keep your hair dry in the shower or when taking a swim.
So when you need a hat visit Sally or Poppy
We'll put a smile on your face that makes you feel happy and hoppy.

So the next time you visit Florida, be sure to visit Poppy's hat shop. Sally and Poppy will be hoppin happy to see you.

Have happy country bed time dreams,
"Grandpa Ed"

33

GRANDPA ED'S BEDTIME STORIES

TRUE BLUE
AND SWAMP GOO

BY JAMES E. MARTIN

TRUE BLUE AND SWAMP GOO

There is a vast marshland called the Everglades which surrounds Lake Okeechobee in the southern part of the state of Florida. Much of the watery swamp land is also covered by dense jungles of vines, sawgrass, cypress trees, scrub pine, Spanish bayonets, and palmetto plants. The swamps are home to many thousands of alligators, panthers, wildcats, foxes, deer, many nasty snakes, and more than a hundred kinds of birds. Nobody knows where they came from, but many years before Florida got its name, there was only one kind of people who lived in the Everglades. They still live there. They call themselves Seminoles, a tribe of American Indians.

The Seminoles live a very simple life style, surviving by hunting, fishing, and gardening for their food. They also raise chickens, pigs, cows, and dogs. Many of their houses are built atop tall poles to protect themselves from the swamp water, the snakes, alligators, and the wild animals. Their houses are kept dry inside by roofing their houses using thick layers of palm leaves.

Most American Indians give their children nature names such as Running Dear, Howling Wolf, White Cloud, Growling Bear, or Shining Star. It is said that Indian fathers usually name their children. Stories are told that when the father leaves the bedroom where the mother and newly born baby lay, he walks outside the house and closes his eyes. He then names the child after the very first thing he sees when he once more opens his eyes. He may see a leaping fawn, a screaming eagle, or a barking dog.

This brings to life the story about a little Seminole boy whose father looked toward the sky to thank The Great Spirit for his baby son only moments after his birth. There was not a cloud in the sky, which at that

35

time was dark blue. The father told The Great Spirit, "My son shall be known as True Blue."

From the time that True Blue was able to walk, he had great love for his home in the Everglades. He tried to follow his father's foot steps where ever he went. True Blue dearly loved his mother, but his father was his greatest hero. True Blue followed his father so closely that, if the man stopped, True Blue bumped into him. When True Blue learned to talk, he tried to talk like his father. When he walked, he tried to walk like his father. He tried to imitate his father's every move and facial expression. He even trained himself to laugh the way his father did. What was even more important, he learned to be honest, and brave, and good just like his father was. His mother Gentle Fawn and Swift Falcon, his father were very proud of their little son.

True Blue grew into a strong healthy youth with dark skin, sparkling black eyes, and glossy black hair that seemed to reflect the bright sun light. Just like his father, True Blue learned the ways of the birds, the fish, the alligators, and the animals who lived in the vast marshlands. Swift Falcon always took his son with him on hunting and fishing trips into the deep jungle. He taught True Blue how to find directions using the sun, the stars, the moon, and the wind. He taught his son how to track both men and animals by even the faintest footprint, broken twig, or disturbed soil. True Blue learned how to find and follow ancient trails. He trained his keen eyes to see the slightest movement both day and night, and to see creatures whose coloring blended in with their surroundings. He learned the calls with which wild creatures communicated with each other, their sounds of joy, as well as their sounds of distress. The swamps and the creatures and plants give off many odors whose messages True Blue learned to understand. He learned which plants, fruits, and nuts were safe to eat so that he could live off the land at times when he was far from home.

True Blue spent so much time exploring the jungles that it became impossible for him to become lost. All of the lessons he learned from his father as well as from his own experiences made him very wise. He always felt at home no matter where he was.

While True Blue was still quite young, his father returned one day from a trip to a large city. The day he returned was True Blue's birthday. His father told True Blue to close his eyes and turn his back, because he had brought his son a birthday surprise. When his mother and father were ready, they told True Blue to face them and open his eyes. What he saw caused him to let out a whoop of joy! His present was a black Labrador Retriever puppy. His joy knew no bounds as he plopped down on the ground and gathered the puppy into his arms as he shouted, "Oh! Thank you. Thank you!" His parents knew that they could not have given him anything else which would have pleased him more.

Labradors are known to love the water, to be strong swimmers, they have strong bodies, and are great hunters. They are also good natured and have great loyalty. The boy and the little puppy became instant friends as they played chase, rolled, and tumbled upon the ground. The mother and father watched the new friends play with great amusement. From that moment onward, True Blue and the puppy were never apart. They even slept in the same bed.

"What are you going to name your dog?" asked True Blue's father.

"I want to wait a few days before I name him," replied True Blue wisely. "I want to be sure that his name will best describe him. I am sure that he will show me what his name should be."

His parents were very proud of True Blue's intelligent answer.

During the next few days, True Blue shared the excitement of exploring the nearby swamps with his new friend. He knew that a small puppy could easily become lost, so until the puppy gained size and strength, they stayed close to home and walked only well worn paths. It was one day when True Blue took the puppy fishing that his little friend showed him what his name should be. Since it is a Labrador's nature to love water, the gawky puppy plopped into the very first mud hole he saw. He splashed and rolled in the muck until he was an awesome mess. His color turned from black into the color of chocolate! The puppy was having so much fun, he seemed to invite True Blue to join him. Well, why not? Soon the boy and his dog were a blur of mud and goo as they wrestled and tossed about in a wild tangle of arms and legs. Needless to say, both the boy and his dog were a slimy mess, covered form end to end with grimy blue swamp goo. They emerged from that swamp looking like some sort of weird swamp monsters as they fell exhausted upon the ground. As the boy lay on his back laughing and looking up at the sky while clutching the very muddy puppy to his chest, the puppy's name came to him right out of the blue.

"Swamp Goo! That's what I'll name him! Swamp Goo!"

The boy was so excited that he did not take time to rinse himself with clean water. He dashed home to tell his parents the exciting news, never giving a thought to how strange that both he and the pup must have appeared. He rushed to where his parents were standing followed closely by the puppy.

"Mother, Father," he shouted. "I have named my puppy Swamp Goo."

"Do I know you?" his mother asked. "You sound like a boy but what kind of a creature are you?"

Both parents were shaking with laughter at the funny sight of the boy and his dog. Between fits of laughter, the parents finally admitted that from the way that puppy looked, there could be no more suitable name for him, so from that day onward the pup's name was Swamp Goo.

Happy times were endless in the warm Florida climate where the youth and his dog could camp out day and night. The two friends wandered ever deeper into the Everglades, learning the secrets of survival and how to find their way back home. Many times they traveled by canoe through the sawgrass and cypress forests, often exploring the Indian River and Lake Okeechobee. For hours they would drift silently in the canoe, the sound broken only by the calls of birds, the yap of a fox, or the deep thunking bellow of an alligator. Sometimes True Blue and his dog would discover the homes of old men called hermits who live alone in the swamps. Their houses were built very much like True Blue's home back in the Indian village. Those old men did not trust strangers, but after True Blue and Swamp Goo visited them for a while, they became good friends. Sometimes True Blue paid each of the old men return visits when he would bring them simple gifts of food and simple medicines. There were times when the visitors would spend several days with their new friends who seemed to enjoy a break in their lonely lives.

Every week or so, True Blue would return home to visit his family and friends. It was good to trade stories with Swift Falcon, to eat some of his Mother's good food, and to catch up on the village news. It was during one of those visits home when True Blue heard something very disturbing over the radio. He learned that a pack of Cub Scouts from one of the large cities had traveled to a park near the Everglades twenty miles from the Indian village where True Blue lived. The Cub Scouts were brought there for a picnic. One of the little scouts had wandered off into the swamps and could not be found. The police and a great number of other people had joined the search for the little boy, but he had not been missed until late in the day, so darkness fell upon the Everglades almost before the search began. Only someone who really knew their way through the vast swampland could avoid becoming lost themselves, even during day light. A night time search would be almost useless. Calls were being made by radio stations for anyone who knew their way through the swamps to please offer their help before it was too late to save the little boy's life.

True Blue heard the call for help. He had never seen a city boy before, but he asked his father if he would allow him to help. His father answered that he would be proud to have his son help someone so badly in need of a friend. Swift Falcon knew a man in the village who owned a small truck. He asked his friend to take True Blue and Swamp Goo to the search headquarters at the park where the little boy had become lost. It was early morning now and the little boy had spent the night lost in the swamp. The men at the search headquarters were busy talking on radios, speaking to helicopter pilots, and sending out search parties. When True Blue offered his help, the policemen said, "Get outta the way kid and get that mangy dog outta here. We don't have time to waste on some ignorant skinny Indian kid with a dog!"

True Blue was deeply hurt, so he called to Swamp Goo to follow him. He quietly entered the edge of the swamp where he heard someone say that the little boy was last seen. True Blue knew that a little boy who was a stranger to the swamps could not live long without food. He also knew that the strength of a little boy would be no match for the difficulty of travel inside the swamp. It was not long before True Blue and his dog had traveled far enough into the jungle that they could no longer hear the sounds of the other searchers. Realizing that he must follow a good plan of search if the hoped to find the little boy, True Blue began to work in half circle sweeps backwards and forwards, always increasing the distance from the park with each pass. Progress was very slow and it seemed that time was quickly running out when True Blue realized that the late afternoon sun had traveled far into the western sky. He and Swamp Goo turned their sensitive ears to hear if the little boy cried for help. Their sharp eyes searched for any trace of trampled weeds or broken twigs. It had grown to be late afternoon and they became very discouraged when, much to their delight, two swamp deer came crashing through the undergrowth almost running over the boy and his dog. True Blue and Swamp Goo dashed excitedly through the swamp in the direction from which the deer has come. Swamp Goo rushed ahead with his keen nose following the trail of the deer. True Blue could hardly believe his eyes when, in their headlong rush, he and his dog crashed into a fallen cypress tree partly hidden from view by thick clumps of palmetto bushes. There sat the little boy out on the log where it rested above a deep pool of water! He was sitting with his feet pulled tightly under him and his arms wrapped around his knees. He was trembling and crying softly. He was so lonely that he hardly noticed when True Blue and Swamp Goo arrived. It seemed that he had given up all hope. His clothing was torn to rags and he had lost both of his shoes in the deep sucking muck of the swamp. His skin was a craze of bloody scratches from the sharp edges of sawgrass and the poisonous barbs of Spanish bayonets. He was tired, scared, and hungry.

True Blue called the little boy's name, which he had learned from the news reports.

"Joey," he said. "My name is True Blue. My dog and I have come to take you home. We want to be your friend. I will climb out to you and you take my hand."

Within seconds, True Blue had reached Joey and carefully guided him to safety upon the ground. There was nothing that True Blue could do to ease Joey's pains, but he gave him water to drink from his canteen and gave him some dried deer jerky to chew upon. The sun was beginning to sink beneath the horizon when True Blue lifted Joey upon his shoulders and began the difficult hike back to the park and the search headquarters.

When they finally arrived, the news reporters and all of the policemen except one and a deputy had gone home. The sheriff in charge of the rescue had called the search off at sundown and had informed Joey's parents that there was no hope of finding him alive. The two men were busy gathering up their equipment and were preparing to leave when True Blue, Swamp Goo, and Joey arrived. The two men could only blink with amazement at the Indian youth standing inside the room with the pitiful little Joey resting astride his shoulders. The policeman was the same one who had told True Blue to get out of his way earlier in the day and to leave the search to men who knew what they were doing. Now he could only fluster in shame as he gawked with open mouthed disbelief at the two soaked and scratched boys covered with mud and a grimy wet dog that smelled liked a grimy wet dog.

The deputy finally found his voice and said, "Here, put the boy down on this couch. Give him some food and water while I call his parents, call a doctor, and recall the rescue squad. Bud, you get on the phone and call the television and radio stations. We have ourselves a real live hero here! You have done a great job, Boy! How on earth did you find him?"

The park was soon becoming crowded once more by people as the good news spread. The people whom True Blue had seen that morning were very sad. This time, the people were happy. As the crowd began to gather, True Blue took advantage of the distraction of people crowding about to get a glimpse of Joey and to shout best wishes to him. True Blue and Swamp Goo quietly slipped away into the darkness and reentered the swamp.

For the first few miles, they traveled along hear the highway, staying out of sight of passing motorists. After awhile, True Blue came across an old familiar trail which lead toward the Indian village. After two days of hiking and sleeping in the Everglades, he and Swamp Goo arrived home.

After True Blue and Swamp Goo left the park headquarters, the news reporters and Joey's parents arrived. At first they were only interested in Joey, but many people, especially Joey's parents began asking what became of the Indian boy who rescued Joey. But the hero was nowhere to be found.

True Blue's proud parents and his friends gave him and Swamp Goo a warm welcome when they arrived home. The whole village celebrated with a great feast. Although the announcers on the radio and television stations as well as many Florida newspapers begged the hero of Joey's rescue to come forward to receive public praise, True Blue was a hero to the only people who really loved him.

"Grandpa Ed"

James E. Martin

James E. Martin

ITCHY TWITCHY – THE SWAMP WUMP

When it is late at night down in the Dismal Swamp, long after the sun goes down, when the day birds have stopped singing, when the frogs are croaking, the crickets are chirping, the moon is beginning to rise, a hush has settled over the land, and little children have gone to bed; that is when a weird creature named Itchy Twitchy, the Swamp Wump emerges from beneath the slimy swamp water and the yukie smelly gray swamp goo. His entire body is covered by coarse stringy green hair which drips with water and mud and is snarled by gobs of swamp grass. He has hands and feet shaped like those of a frog, but his body is shaped like a large gorilla. His legs are bowed and short, but his arms are so long that his knuckles touch the ground as he walks stooped over like an old old man. His eyes stare from beneath great bushy eyebrows.

Itchy Twitchy always sits upon his favorite large rock near the edge of the swamp where he enjoys watching the yellow moon rise. He also enjoys listening to the bugs chirp, the night birds cry, and bull frogs croak. He, himself, cannot croak, chirp, or sing. Nor can he speak. He can, however, make a loud bellowing sound form which he gets his name. He goes WHUMP! WHUMP! WHUMP! Sometimes he can hear his echo coming back to him from across the huge swamp and the sound amuses him. At those times, he laughs a hideous loud laugh YEEE AH HAW HAW! The sound is so terrible that all of the bugs, birds, and frogs become silent from fear. When the other creatures become silent, Itchy Twitchy becomes very sad. You see, Itchy Twitchy is one of a kind. He is all alone, because he has no family or friends. He does not know where he came from. He would like to become friends with the bugs, the birds, and the frogs, but he is so large and ugly, all of the other creatures are afraid of him. When he laughs, they do not understand, so they become more afraid of him.

Itchy Twitchy's sadness becomes so great that it causes him to have a nervous reaction. Due to the very unsanitary conditions in which he lives deep down in the swamp muck, his skin if very filthy. When he gets nervous, his skin breaks out in hives (which you know become very itchy, if you have ever had them). When Itchy Twitchy became itchy, he also became very twitchy. The more he itched, the more he twitched. The more he twitched, the more he itched. When he could endure the discomfort no longer, he sadly returned beneath the swamp where the cool water soothed his tortured skin. After he went away, the bugs, and birds, the crickets, and the frogs began to sing to the yellow moon which had risen high into the sky.

Now Alice was a sweet little girl who was in the second grade in school. She and many of her classmates had to rise so early in the morning to catch the school bus, they became very sleepy during the long afternoon after lunch. Mrs. Polk, their teacher, realized that sleepy students could not learn very well, if they could not stay awake.

So each afternoon when the class returned from lunch, she allowed them to rest their heads upon their desk tops to take a fifteen minute nap. Of course there is no animal called a Swamp Wump, but it was during one of Alice's afternoon naps that she had a dream about Itchy Twitchy. As you know, fifteen minutes is not very long, so Mrs. Polk awakened her before she finished her dream. Now she must forever wonder what became of poor Itchy Twitchy.

Some of her questions were: How did he happen to be the only animal of his kind? Where did he come from? Why did he choose to live beneath the swamp in the first place? How could he live beneath the swamp? Was there some sort of magic happening here? Could it be that he was some unfortunate little boy upon which some wicked gnome had cast a spell? If so, how could someone break the spell and return him to his parents? What could be a happy ending to Alice's dream?

James E. Martin

Hey! You children know the ways of elves, and witches, trolls, and gnomes. I'll bet you could help me write a happy ending to Alice's story. If you could draw your idea of what a swamp wump looked like, take it home with you, and tell your parents the story of Alice's dream, maybe they would help you finish it. For you see, your parents were wee people just like you a long time ago. They, too, once lived in a world of wee people and magic. If you can think of a way to free poor Itchy Twitchy, perhaps you could send me your happy ending by writing to Grandpa Ed Martin, c/o Department of Bed Time Stories, HC 30, Box 183, Caldwell, West Virginia 24925.

With oodles of county love,
Your Friend, Grandpa Ed

These are some of the answers I have received:

One afternoon when Alice got out of school, she went down by the swamp. She sat down and watched the yellow moon rise into the sky. Then she waited to see Itchy Twitchy rise up and, when he did, they became best friends. When she hugged him, he was his normal self.

LAUREN ASBURY
Second Grade, White Sulphur Springs Elementary School 1997

* * * * *

One day Itchy Twitchy, The Swamp Wump, went to his favorite Rock and he sang his favorite song over and over and over. He Sang "rippet" "rippet". The end.

KELLEA COLE
White Sulphur Springs Elementary School 1997
Mrs. Gillian's Second Grade Class

* * * * *

46

So one day the little girl went to the swamp and looked for him and then she found him. She and him were looking in their eyes and she kissed him and he turned to a man and they lived happy ever after. The end

AUTUMN FRALEY
White Sulphur Springs Elementary School 1997
Mrs. Polk's Second grade Class

* * * * *

Suddenly Alice heard a sound coming from the closet in her bedroom. She quickly ran down stairs. Following her was Itchy Twitchy. Suddenly he started to change into a young boy named Joe.

THOMAS TAYLOR
Second Grade White Sulphur Spring Elementary School 1997

Itchy Twitchy, The Swamp Wump, needs to come up out of the swamp and try nicely to talk to birds and all the animals. Tell why he is dirty and why he itches and twitches. Alice and her classmates could go to the swamp, help the animals to see that Itchy Twitchy isn't so bad.

DANIELLE HOKE
White Sulphur Springs Elementary School 1997
Mrs. Moran's Third Grade Class

She (Alice) makes a magical pochen and goes to the swamp and turns Itchy Twitchy to a boy.

JAKE ARNOLDT
Whites Sulphur Springs Elementary 1997
Mrs. Moran's Third Grade Class

As soon as Little Alice got up from her nap, she ate her snack. Later Alice went home. When she got home, she started thinking about Itchy Twitchy. She really wanted to help him and to cheer him up. When it was time for bed, Little Alice went to sleep, she started to dream about Itchy Twitchy, but Itchy Twitchy was still very sad and lonesome. Alice just had to help him, so she took a walk down to the swamp where Itchy Twitchy lived.

"Itchy Twitchy! Itchy Twitchy!" Alice called.

He finally came up, but with a very sad face.

"Hi, Itchy Twitchy! How are you today?" she asked. He only groaned. "How I wish I could help him", she said to herself.

"Hey, Itchy Twitchy, can you do me a favor?" she asked.

Itchy Twitchy groaned once more and answered, "Yes-s-s, I guess-s-s-. What is it?"

"Will you sing a little song with me?" continued Alice.

"I guess", groaned Itchy Twitchy. "What is it?"

"It is called "Over The Hills", replied Alice. "Now lets hit it. A one and a two. A one two three four. Over the river and through the woods to Grandmother's house we go."

They sang it over and over, on and on. That started the frogs to singing; the grasshoppers and birds began to sing. That cheered him up. It made Itchy Twitchy even happier when Little Alice said, "Let's sing it some more. On the count of four, hit it!"

Alice was so proud of herself now that she had made Itchy Twitchy happy. From that time onward, Itchy Twitchy sang his song of happiness with his swamp friends and overcame his sadness.

TANYA KING
White Sulphur Springs
Elementary School 1997
Mrs. White's Sixth Grade Class

Late one evening as Itchy Twitchy emerged from the swamp waters and began to sit on his favorite rock, he noticed something he had never seen before. He saw two bright lights coming in his direction and stop nearby. Being curious, he slowly walked toward the lights and stopped suddenly when he saw two creatures that seemed to be speaking to one another. Even more surprising to Itchy was that he could understand what the creatures were saying. He listened as the bigger creature talked to the smaller one. It was saying how he and a friend had come to this very spot many years ago. They were frog hunting for a science experiment that was to be a blue ribbon winner. They had been combining the blood of several animals to create a new animal.

The speaker said, "We had just taken blood from a frog and had mixed it with the blood of a gorilla and a pig, which we already had, when my friend slipped in a green puddle of slime. He jumped up screaming with

49

the blood and slime all over him. He ran blindly into the swamp and was never seen again. I would have done anything to help my friend."

Then, out of the corner of her eye, the smaller creature noticed Itchy Twitchy standing in the moonlight. Itchy Twitchy being in a daze upon hearing the sad tale of the friends, did not notice the two creatures approaching him. The bigger creature could not believe what he was seeing; a mutated form of a gorilla or something. He wondered if it could be, by some miracle his long lost friend. Being a doctor, he asked his wife, the smaller creature, to bring his medical bag from the car. When she returned, he removed a syringe and drew some of his own human blood into it. He slowly approached Itchy Twitchy, speaking to him calmly.

Itchy Twitchy, who had been so lonely for so long, found himself being afraid and wanting to run away, but for some unknown reason, he did not. The doctor gave Itchy, The Swamp Wump a shot of his own blood and watched with amazement as a miraculous event occurred. Hair began falling from the swamp wump and his frog feet and hands became human. Yes, it was true that Itchy was his old friend. Itchy was human once more and was no longer lonely. The two friends were happy once more and remained friends to this very day.

STUDENT DID NOT LIST HIS NAME.
White Sulphur Springs Elementary School 1996
Believed to be Jarrod Fleshman; Mrs. Ramsey's Sixth Grade Class

A good fairy turned Itchy Twitchy into a frog, because he was so unhappy. The other animals were excited because he was now a frog, and no longer ugly and scary. Itchy Twitchy was happy, too. Now he had friends and was not alone. He lived happily ever after with the other animals.

LEANN CHILDERS
White Sulphur Springs Elementary School 1997
Mrs. Polk's Second Grade Class

That night after school, Alice decided to go for a walk in the woods. Soon it became dark. Alice could not see where she was going. Suddenly, she fell into a swamp. She fell so fast into the deep swamp, she could not call for help. Suddenly, she was being carried out of the water. When she was on land, she looked to see what was carrying her. She was very frightened at first, but she realized that this monster had been in her dream. It was Itchy Twitchy. Itchy Twitchy handed her a piece of paper that was ripped and muddy. Alice read the words out loud and, suddenly, Itchy Twitchy turned into a boy about Alice's age. Alice was shocked. Itchy Twitchy explained that when he was little, his parents died and a witch turned him into a swamp wump. Alice asked him where he would live. He said that he didn't know. Then Alice said that he could live with her and her family. Itchy said, "OK". When it became light, Itchy Twitchy and Alice went home.

SAVANNAH BURNS
Sixth Grade, White Sulphur Springs Elementary School 1997

One morning, the crickets taught Itchy Twitchy to chirp. That afternoon, the birds taught him to sing. That evening, the frogs taught him to croak. They all became friends and formed a Rock n' Roll band named Itchy Twitchy and The Swamp Wumps.

James E. Martin

KATE BOWLING
As dictated to her Mother
White Sulphur Springs Elementary School 1997
Mrs. Polk's Second Grade Class

GRANDPA ED'S BEDTIME STORIES

HENRY COMES TO THE COUNTRY

BY JAMES E. MARTIN

James E. Martin

HENRY COMES TO THE COUNTRY

Henry came into being in a big city called Detroit, Michigan in the year 1923. Henry was an automobile named after his inventor, a very rich and intelligent man, Mr. Henry Ford. Please understand that Henry was only one of many thousands of cars built by Mr. Ford's factory workers. You might say that Henry had many brothers and sisters scattered throughout the United States of America.

Henry was a very special automobile in many ways. He was by no means the oldest member of his family, but he was the product of an unusual new idea began by Mr. Ford called mass production by using an assembly line. That means that each worker along the assembly line had a single item to install on the car being built as a conveyor belt moved it slowly past his work station on its way to the finish line. Until Mr. Ford introduced his new idea, very few cars existed anywhere in the world. Most people were still using horses for transportation by riding upon their backs, using them to pull buggies, wagons, or stage coaches. Automobiles that did exist were hand made in small shops. Hardly any two of them were alike and most were very unreliable playthings owned by only the very wealthy.

The horse and buggy society of that time in America did not like automobiles very much, because the engines made strange noises. Many times, the engines also backfired making a sound like a cannon shot. That noise often caused horses to become frightened. Many times they threw their riders or ran out of control causing the vehicles they were pulling to wreck and injure the passengers. As the number of automobiles increased, many towns enacted laws to prevent them from using the streets. One law in Charleston, West Virginia stated that if a driver intended to enter certain streets, he must send a man on foot one hundred yards ahead shouting, "Warning! There's a car coming! There's a car coming!"

Being rich as he was, Mr. Ford traveled throughout the world aboard steam ships and by railroad. He observed the production of the world's finest cars in many countries. He noticed that the process was very slow and that only a few cars could be built every year. He returned to America with a great new idea. He built a large factory where he mass produced thousands of duplicate parts and hired thousands of mechanics to build hundreds of cars each day on the assembly line. Instead of charging extremely high prices for his cars, he priced them at only a few hundreds of dollars so that, not only the wealthy, but almost everyone could afford to buy one. The mechanics who built the cars could also afford to buy them, so Mr. Ford not only created the factory to build his cars, but also created his own market among his employees! Soon every manufacturer in the world was copying Mr. Ford's ideas of mass production.

Mr. Ford put the finest materials and workmanship into his cars. They were the finest cars in the world. They ran smoothly and were very dependable. What is more, the engines were quieted through the use of a muffler. Everyone wanted a T-Model Ford!

Ah! Old Henry was a handsome fellow! He had a glossy black body shaped like a bathtub. It had four metal doors that were high enough where people could rest their elbows on top of them in comfort. Henry had two wide seats both front and back made with well padded deep coils and covered with black canvas. The back seat was elevated slightly higher than the front seat to enable the rear seat passengers to have a clear view of the road. The body was covered with a padded canvas top stretched over a tubular frame that could be folded down if desired. The T-Models were among the first cars on earth to have a glass windshield. The car was powered by a wonderful little four cylinder engine, the finest of its day. Night time lighting was provided by two large brass bound electric headlights enabling the Fords to travel at night. Old Henry was supported by four wooden spoked wheels painted beautiful black with yellow stripes.

Henry made the long journey from Detroit to Rainelle, West Virginia aboard a railroad box car. His new owner had paid eight hundred fifty dollars for him and was anxious to take him home. The man's name was Tom and his wife was Rachel. They lived on a mountain farm eight miles from town. On the day, they had ridden to town with a neighbor so that they could drive their new car home.

The owner of the Ford dealership had Old Henry ready when his new owners arrived. He had given Henry a bath and had filled the gasoline tank. Tom had never driven a car, so it was necessary for the dealer to take Tom and Rachel to a large level field where he could safely teach Tom how to drive Henry. After practicing for an hour or two, Tom was able to drive reasonably well, so they returned to the dealership. The dealer wished them good luck and they began the trip over the rutted dirt road to the farm. Of course, Tom was somewhat nervous as anyone would be driving a strange vehicle for the first time.

Everything went well for the first few miles on that sunny afternoon. Tom and Rachel were enjoying themselves very much as they passed the homes of friends and gave a loud "ooogah' sound of greeting with Old Henry's claxon horn. Tom was accustomed to traveling in a horse drawn buggy, so he was careful not to drive faster than a few miles per hour. At a distance of three miles out of town, they came to a first steep hill. Henry climbed the grade without difficulty, but the downgrade once they reached the top was extremely steep. That was going to be Tom's first serious test of his ability to control Henry. He selected the lowest gear and slowly descended the hill. As Henry began to gain speed, however, Tom began to panic. If Henry had one weakness it was that he didn't have very effective brakes. Near the bottom of that hill, there was a sharp curve to the left. By the time they arrived at that curve, Henry was moving much faster than Tom was accustomed to when riding a horse drawn wagon. He may have been able to make the curve safely had the front wheels not dropped into a deep rut. The steering wheel gave a violent spin right out of Tom's grasp.

Henry lunged hard to the right tossing Tom out over the top of the door on the driver's side and began to leave the narrow road and upset on his side while sliding down an embankment into a small ravine. Poor Tom was scared out of his wits as he regained his feet and rushed across the road and slid down the embankment to where Henry lay with all wheels pointed skyward.

Tom worked his way around Henry so that he could clamber up the ravine and look into the passenger compartment where Rachel was still trying with great difficulty to turn herself right side up.

"Are you alright, Rachel?" asked Tom as he tried to catch his breath. "Yes, thank you," replied Rachel, "But I think that my neck's broke!"

Tom and Rachel clawed their way up the side of the ravine with some difficulty and returned to the road where they evaluated their scratches and bruises. They were fortunate that their injuries were very slight, but their clothing was torn and dirty. It was only a short distance to a neighbor's house where they went for help. The neighbor's wife comforted Rachel and helped her to clean and treat her scratches. The neighbor man and some of other men took a team of horses and accompanied Tom back to the scene of the accident. Fortunately, the ravine had an open end which made it rather easy to tow Henry to a point where he could re-enter the roadway. It did not require much effort to tilt the car back onto its wheels. Aside from some scratches on the side of his beautifully painted black body, Henry had suffered very little damage. After checking fluid levels of the engine, the men had very little trouble getting Henry's motor started. After thanking their neighbors for their kind assistance, Tom and Rachel resumed their trip homeward. The happy mood of the earlier part of the trip in their new car was gone now and they wondered if they had made a bad mistake buying Henry.

That had been a very eventful day and it was late afternoon when the travelers arrived home. Tom easily guided Henry down the fence lined lane leading to their farm house. Tom had built a new shed on the side of his barn as a home for Henry. The barn was a short distance further down the lane past the farm house and beyond a gate which had to be opened. Tom had driven horses pulling a wagon down that lane many times during his lifetime. Just at this moment, however, Tom's mind was daydreaming and, as he had so many times before when approaching the gate, Tom said, "Woah! Woah!"

Shouting Woah would have worked very well for horses, but had absolutely no effect whatsoever on Henry. He sent splinters flying in all directions as he crashed through the gate, knocking off both headlights as he went! In the excitement, Tom was still yelling Whoa! As Henry rammed into the side of the barn and buried his radiator into the wall with a jolting stop!

Poor Tom and Rachel! They were so bewildered that they didn't know what to do. And poor Henry! Look at him. He was a total mess. The following day, Tom hired a neighbor to help him repair Henry's shed and to put Henry inside his new home.

Henry's first trip to the country was his only trip, because Tom never drove Henry again.

"Grandpa Ed"

GRANDPA ED'S BEDTIME STORIES

MR TWIT

BY JAMES E. MARTIN

MORTIMER TWIT

James E. Martin

MR. TWIT

He was a strange one, that Mr. Twit. He would not talk, so the town's people would never have learned his name if they had not read it on the side of his suitcase. His arrival in the town of Blizzard, Montana was quite a mystery. He must have arrived late at night while the people of Blizzard were asleep. No one seemed to know how he arrived. Perhaps he was a hobo who rode into town on a late night freight train, or maybe he walked.

There was something else which added to the mystery. It was not unusual for the town of Blizzard to have some terrible winter weather. That was how the town got its name, but on the night of Mr. Twit's arrival, the town of Blizzard was having one of the worst snow storms in its history. Schools had been closed for days and all traffic had stopped on the highways. Mail was not being delivered, electric power had failed, and dairy farmers in the countryside had been pouring their milk upon the ground, because all of their tanks were full and they could not get the milk to market. Everything was at a standstill. It would be hard to imagine a worse time, even for Blizzard.

When daylight came that morning, the town's mayor, the town policemen, and the firemen all came to their offices at city hall moving afoot with great difficulty through the deep snow and howling wind. Each person was so focused upon their own difficulty walking that they hardly noticed any one else along the way. It was only after they were safely inside their offices that they looked out of their windows to see if any one else was moving along the street. That was when the mayor noticed a man dimly visible through the swirling snow. He was standing on the lawn in front of city hall facing the town square as though he was a tourist who was viewing the town for the very first time. The mayor called the policemen and firemen into his office and asked,

"Who is that man standing out there on the lawn?"

"Why, that poor man!" exclaimed the fire chief as he dashed out of City Hall followed closely by the chief of police.

Mr. Twit was standing atop a small knoll where the wind had swept the snow completely away exposing the bare ground. Mr. Twit's suitcase rested upon the ground beside his left leg. He, himself, was frozen stiff. He actually resembled a life-sized statue. He wore a black derby styled

60

hat upon his head with a velvet cord attached and tied under his chin to prevent the hat from blowing away. He wore red fuzzy ear muffs to protect his ears. He wore a white shirt with great curly ruffles at his wrists and around the collar, the kind of shirt worn by a riverboat gambler. His suit coat which was unbuttoned down the front was made of thick jet black velvet. The edges of the coat lapels and down the front edges were trimmed with golden yellow piping. Beneath the coat, he wore a glittery vest whose color alternated in a fancy design between ebony black and brilliant gold. Opposite ends of a heavy gold watch chain with fancy square links draped across his portly stomach. His hands were covered inside grey suede gloves, his right hand gripping the top of a fancy black walking cane, the end of which was firmly planted into the frozen ground. His grey trousers contained long black stripes which ran lengthwise from his waist to his ankles. Upon his feet, he wore shiny black patent leather shoes with sharp pointed toes over which and around his ankles he wore spats made of snow white canvas.

The firemen and policemen soon discovered that Mr. Twit was firmly frozen to the ground. His entire body was as rigid as stone. His long pointed nose was his only facial feature which contained any color. Its tip was sort of orange or red. The remainder of his face was as white as frost. Even his pencil thin mustashe and black eyebrows were covered by frost. His curly black hair stuck out from under his hat from all sides. His dark eyes stared straight ahead as though they saw nothing. There was absolutely no hope that Mr. Twit was alive. With all of the firemen and policemen tugging upon Mr. Twit, try as they may, they could not budge him from the frozen ground. What was worse, the storm grew colder and the snow kept falling.

All the while, Mr. Twit continued to stand beside his suitcase upon the city hall lawn. The news of his discovery became known far and wide across the land once electrical power was restored and news broadcasts told of a strange well dressed man frozen like stone stood on the city hall lawn of Blizzard, Montana. Towns folk, photographers, reporters, and country people riding snow mobiles came from miles around to see the frozen man dressed in fancy clothes who nobody knew.

The winter weather remained extremely cold for many days, during which Mr. Twit remained firmly frozen in place. The town officials pondered as to how Mr. Twit could be moved without breaking off his legs. All agreed that, since Mr. Twit was so thoroughly frozen, no further harm could come to him by leaving him there until the weather began to get warmer. So there he stood day after day looking out upon the square, his secret identity locked inside his suitcase.

Suddenly, during the night of March 31, without warning whatsoever, while all of Blizzard's townspeople slept in their beds, the night air became very warm. A real heatwave. When the people of city hall came to work, Mr. Twit was gone never to be seen again! All that remained where Mr. Twit stood were his fancy clothes and his suitcase, inside on a sheet of white paper written in large black letters were the words 'APRIL FOOL!' For you see, Mr. Twit was only a cleverly crafted snowman!

Can you imagine the red faces for miles around? Well, snowmen do not just happen. Somebody has to build them. Now, actually there were two mischievous very much alive 'Little Twits' who lived in Blizzard. Their names were Tammy and Timmy. Not only were they sister and brother, they were seven year old twins. Their Mommy and Daddy owned a theatrical costume business in Blizzard. Their parents owned many hundreds of costumes which they rented out to playhouses throughout many states.

Tammy and Timmy often dressed in elaborate costumes, pretending that they were famous actors. Their's was a treasure house for young imaginative minds, besides the twins loved to play pranks on their parents and friends. They thought how much fun it would be to see so many adults going ga ga over a silly snowman such as Mr. Twit. By using theatrical supplies, they carefully designed him to look real one night when the whole town was asleep. They dressed him to reveal very little snow. That which did show was tinted to look like someone who was totally frozen. Had the adults only taken the time to notice during all of the flustering and trying to solve the mystery of Mr. Twit, they would have observed two twittering giggling little twins lurking in the background enjoying their April Fool prank.

GRANDPA ED'S BEDTIME STORIES

WHO-O-O-O?

BY JAMES E. MARTIN

James E. Martin

WHO-O-O-O?

Nobody seemed to know when that old brick house had been built. There were people living in that community who were more than eighty years old and had spent their entire lives there. They said that the old house was standing empty when they were children. It must have been well built to last all of those years without repair. People who lived in the neighborhood were afraid to go any closer than the road which passed in front of it. Even then, they stopped talking and hurried past either day or night. As far back as people remembered, the old house was said to be haunted. There was one thing for certain, nobody was in a hurry to find out!

If your were looking for a house that looked goose-bumpy and spooky, that old house would be a good choice. To begin with, the house was located one hundred yards from the road in the center of a swampy four acre field. The neighbors called the property 'Swampy Gables'. The entire lot was surrounded by a rusty wrought iron fence which was overgrown by clusters of maple and elm trees whose lower branches touched the ground in may places, giving the place a ghostly enchanted appearance. The upper parts of the trees were scraggly in their shape against the skyline with their bodies entangled with many years accumulation of storm damaged dead limbs. There were also clusters of trees growing around the house, the limbs of which overhung the roof. Tall weeds and briars grew in large clumps throughout the lawn. Glass was missing from most of the windows which were now dangling in disrepair. Many years accumulation of spiderwebs had grown so long that they waved like dirty curtains through the window openings when the wind blew. One sheet of metal roofing remained attached to the roof by one corner; it made an eerie creaking sound with the force of each passing breeze.

Just to look at that old house caused chills to flitter up and down one's spine. Even dogs whimpered and tucked their tails between their legs when they came near. After dark on most nights, a scary sound came from inside the house. It was a who-o-o! sound. That was enough to cause the bravest of people to hurry away as fast as they could go. Some of the oldest people who lived in the community were told when they were young that an extremely old man was the last person to live in that house.

They said that he lived alone, being known as what is called a hermit. The old man did not like other people and wanted to be left alone. His only friends were a gang of cats. Since he survived upon the food he grew in his garden and was not visited by any other person, he was seldom seen and was never spoken to. For that reason, no one ever knew what happened to the old man. Did he go away or did her perish right there in that old house? When neighbors tried to visit the old man, they were chased away by gun fire, so they simply quit trying to be his friend.

That old house never ceased to be the subject of conversation for miles around. Every so often, some one boasted that he had enough courage to visit the old house. Even some of the husky lads from the local high school football team, trying to impress other students with how brave they were, said that they were going to spend a night sleeping inside the old house. But boast as they may, year after year passed and nobody was brave enough to approach the old house, even during daytime. In the meantime, the eerie sound of who-o-o came from inside the old house.

As years passed, old folk would sit up late at night telling wide eyed children about scary noises that they had heard coming from that old house. They would also tell about seeing lights flickering through the windows on dark stormy nights, about hearing cats squalling as though they were being tortured, and of swarms of huge bats flying out of the house at night almost knocking people's hats off as they walked along the road in front of the place. That house definitely was not a place for the timid or weak of heart to visit.

So the weeds grew taller, the trees almost hid the house from view, the carriage house and other outbuildings sagged and rotted down. Their ruins were overgrown by vines and shrubbery their outlines resembling hooded stoop shouldered monks lurking in the deep shadows. Long wisps of

Spanish moss draped from the bottom limbs of the mangled trees. The entire scene was foreboding during daylight, but with the arrival of darkness, especially during a storm, that house was where nobody would want to be.

Well, not exactly. You see, bravery does not always come in large packages. Sometimes bravery grows out of plain common sense. Common sense is not always found in 'grown-ups' who lack courage themselves and try to scare little kids. Many times, little children just as you are have been blessed with great powers of bravery. Some small kids who believed that there is a logical explanation for everything that happens refused to believe all of those yarns about the house being haunted. This is what happened.

Many children love the adventure of creating their Own Club. Perhaps some of you have done the very same thing. Some build their club in tree houses, some build a shack in the forest, others use an abandoned house as a meeting place. Of course, they always like to surround themselves with a sense of adventure and mystique. It is always more interesting to think up imaginary scenes such as the days of Robin Hood, Sir Lanslot, King Arthur, or Tarzan. This is what is called 'make believe' and it is fun.

Three little boys named Jake, Billy, and George were very best of friends. They also had another very best friend. She was a little girl named Bridget. Bridget was what is known as a 'tomboy'. That means that she likes to play with boys and can do anything that the boys can do. The four of them had another best friend. It was Jake's Spaniel dog named 'Mutt'. Those second grade friends were looking for a suitable place to establish a Club, but had to consider how little money they had to buy materials. They also had to decide upon the best location where it would be out of 'grown-ups' way, where they would have exclusive access to it, and where there would be a sense of mystery and adventure surrounding it.

Tomboy Bridget had a splendid idea – why not use the old haunted house?

"Wow!", everyone shouted at once. "What a great idea!"

Yeah! That would make a swell Club. There would be nothing to build, it would be a place surrounded by mystery, and no one would object to their using it. Walking beneath the tangled trees would be like walking through the Sherwood Forest, the dense grapevines and Spanish moss would be like walking through Tarzan's jungles, and they would imagine the old house as being King Arthur's castle. What a wonderful place for a club it would be! All that remained to be done was give their Club a name and to take possession of it in the name of King Arthur!

Billy said, "Lets call it 'Club Shangra-la!"

"What a great name!", the others all shouted at once.

All that remained to be decided was when they could visit their new Club Headquarters. What an exciting adventure that was going to be! The children had to attend school, after which they also had chores to do after coming home from school. For that reason, it would be necessary for them to make their first visit to the old house at night. They agreed upon which night they all could be present. Each one borrowed a good flashlight from their parents, and, along with dog Mutt, they went to the front gate of the old house. There it stood dark, shadowy, and foreboding.

George said, "I want to be the first to go through the gate. I am Sir Lanslot. I will draw my trusty sword. I do not know the meaning of fear!"

Old Mutt did not act as though he was very enthusiastic about the whole idea. He sort of whimpered and hung back, but he was determined that he would not abandon his friends no matter what happened. So one after another, the friends worked their way through the drapes of Spanish moss and tangled branches of the trees. It was not long before they heard the eerie sound of "Who-o-o! Who-o-o! coming from inside the house. The children stopped and looked at each other as though to take a 'bravery check', but once more George began creeping through the tall weeds toward the house. Suddenly a swarm of bats attracted by the bright beams of the flashlights went swirling past the children's heads.

Bridget swatted at them with a wave of her arm and shouted with disgust, "Shoo! Go away! You keep going George," she said.

The swirling of the bats gave Old Mutt new courage as he made leaping attempts to catch them as they swooshed past. By this time, Sir George 'Lanslot' had reached the bottom of the rickety old front porch steps. One by one, each of the club members climbed the steps and paused breathlessly outside the massive oak door. It was almost half way open, hanging by only a bottom hinge. Beyond the sagging door loomed the eerie darkness inside the house where no human eye had viewed for more than eighty years. George handed Billy his flashlight in order that he could use two hands to lift the heavy door into an open position. As the door moved, the rusty hinge emitted a nasty spooky screeching sound, which startled several cats to noisily escape through open windows with Old Mutt in hot pursuit. The children could not help breaking out in an uproar of laughter because of that unexpected clamor. With the door now wide open, all four children crowded through. They were standing inside a large room with ceilings that must have been twelve feet high. Bats flew in circles inside the room as though it were a cave. Shrouds of cobwebs dangled from every corner with the spiders scampering to shield themselves from the beams of bright light. As the lights were aimed about the room, they all came to focus upon the mantel above a large smoke-stained stone fireplace. In front of a picture frame almost four feet square containing the faded painting of a fierce looking old man sat the mystery of the who-o-o who-o-o sounds. Sitting there atop the mantel upon a nest made of sticks and reeds was a very large hoot owl! When the light beams met her enormous glaring green eyes, the children's hearts almost stopped with panic. The owl's eyes glowed like some type of weird light bulbs containing spirals. The owl was just as surprised as the children, whose mouths gaped open in amazement. She sat rigidly in place in the glare of the unfamiliar light seeming not to know what to do. She expressed her surprise by voicing a couple of loud hoots before finally taking flight through an open window and disappearing into the night. Once more the children clung to each other in laughter. Boy-e-e! It certainly looked as though having a Club was going to be fun!

After having chased all of the cats up into the trees, Old Mutt joined his friends inside the house once more. The friends explored the kitchen and other rooms on the ground floor. Beneath an eighty year layer of dust, everything was in place just as though the owner had gone away from home that very day. The children climbed the stairs and visited each of four bedrooms of which had furniture in place. The last area to be explored was the basement.

The children were too wise for all four of them to enter the basement at the same time and take a chance of the door closing in a locked position trapping them inside. If that should happen, no one would know where to find them. While Bridget and Billy remained at the top of the stairs, George and Jake descended the basement stairs. Before they had a chance to explore the basement, they froze in their tracks! At the foot of the stairs where he had fallen, lay the fully clothed skeleton of the poor old hermit. The children were saddened as they quietly closed the basement door and returned home to tell their parents about the poor old man.

The following day, hundreds of people came to the old house to watch as the hermit's skeleton was taken away for burial. The residents of the community marveled at how brave the four little friends and their dog were to enter that dreadful old house, especially at night. They became everyone's heroes. Since nobody really owned the old house, Shangra-la became the children's Club House where they and many more of their friends converted the property into a community playground.

James E. Martin

MY FRIEND HOWDY

On an early spring day, Grandpa Ed was in his garden shop starting to clean his tools. Soon it would be time to plant flowers and vegetables. He wanted his tools to be ready for the work ahead. He was standing with his back toward a stack of lumber when he thought that he heard a muffled voice. Grandpa looked about inside the shop, but did not see anyone. He walked outside the shop and then all the way around it, but saw nobody. He returned to inside the shop thinking that his imagination was playing tricks on him. Just as soon as he started working, he heard a voice say, "Hey! Let me out of here!"

Once more the voice sounded muffled as though it were coming from a deep well. Grandpa started walking toward the shop door once more when the voice said, "No! Over here in the lumber stack."

Grandpa is a kind man who is always ready to help anyone who is in trouble. At this moment, however, he was feeling just a little bit huffy, because he thought that someone was trying to make him look like a fool. He asked in a gruff voice, "Where in tarnation are ya? Stop that foolishness and show yourself!"

"Down here", the voice answered. "Get some of this lumber off me! It's squeezing the life outta me."

Grandpa began moving boards from the stack as fast as he could, fearing that someone was in great pain. He couldn't help wondering how anyone could get into such a "fix". Now Grandpa is old, but he can still remember many years ago when he was a very young boy, that his imagination lead him to believe that there were magic "wee people" such as leprechauns, fairies, trolls, and gnomes. They lived in strange places and did strange things. Grandpa always believes that even though he is very old, some of the little boy remains within him. And, after all, he dearly loves children. How could he help but believe that the "wee people" are real?

When Grandpa picked a board that was eight feet long, two inches thick, and ten inches wide, the voice yelled in a cranky, complaining tone, "Put me down! Whew! It sure did take you long enough! Where have you been all winter?"

"Who are you? Where are you?" Grandpa demanded, now more irritated than ever.

71

"What's the matter with you?" the voice scolded. "You are holding me in your hand. My name is Howdy. I'm a scarecrow. I'm trapped in this stupid board. If you will cut me out, I promise to be your faithful friend and I'll scare the crows out of you garden. But please hurry, I can't stand this cramped space any longer."

"You poor fellow," said the kind old man, "But how can I free you when I cannot see you?"

"You're gonna have to saw me out," said Howdy.

The very thought of doing that caused Grandpa to break out with sweat.

How can I cut out what I cannot see? How will I know if I am cutting off your nose or your ears? Oh, this is dreadful! Dreadful!" he said, wringing his hands.

You start by making a mark with a pencil. Each time the pencil touches me, I'll tell you to back off until you have outlined my entire picture. Then all that you will have to do is be careful. But please hurry!" Howdy replied.

Grandpa began work at once drawing lines upon the board with a pencil. He outlined Howdy's face and ears, his head and eyes and hair. Then he began tracing his body. As Grandpa finished outlining Howdy's arms and began drawing along his ribs, Howdy began to giggle and shouted, "Hey, take it easy! You are tickling my laughing place!"

It was not long before Grandpa finished tracing the entire picture of Howdy Scarecrow. Soon Grandpa cut him free of that awful board. Howdy immediately sprang to his feet and began dancing about the shop. He grabbed an old broom and began making wide sweeping motions through the air shouting "Shoo! Shoo! Shoo!" as he pretended to scare imaginary crows. Grandpa had to duck to avoid being struck by the broom, but the only things that Howdy scared were Grandpa's two cats, Skeeter and Sputnik.

"Now cut that out!" yelled Grandpa, "Or I'll put you back inside that board. Besides, you are not wearing any clothing."

I'm sorry" said Howdy. "I am so glad to be free of that board and to get on with my life's work, that I became carried away. You must understand, I have been locked up inside that board for years. Shoo! Shoo! Shoo!" he continued as he shadow boxed about the inside of the shop.

"Now stop that!" shouted Grandpa once more. "Control yourself while I round up some old clothing for you fit for a fine scarecrow such as yourself".

Grandpa went into his house and returned with a shirt, trousers, socks, shoes, suspenders, and a straw hat. Old Howdy was so proud of his new clothing he was fit to pop. Grandpa noticed that Howdy had grown quite pale after being locked up inside that board for so many years, so he gave Howdy some face paint and a comb so that he could tidy his tangled yellow hair. He also gave Howdy a large tobacco pipe to hold in his mouth and a garden hoe to hold in his hand. Howdy was anxious to start to work. I want to tell you, that was one proud scarecrow that went into the garden with Grandpa to take his duty position. Grandpa showed him where he wanted him to stand. He patted Howdy on the shoulder and said, "Good luck."

Howdy set right to work trying to look fierce and mean. He raised his left arm above his head and began saying, "Shoo! Shoo!" but, before Grandpa had time to walk back to his shop, the biggest, blackest crow that Grandpa has even seen alighted upon Howdy's right shoulder, almost knocking his hat off! Grandpa paused with a moment of amusement before entering the door of his shop. He smiled as he watched Howdy shouting, "Shoo! Shoo!" as he tried to scare the crow off his shoulder. Grandpa was thinking, "We have a wonderful life here at Resume Speed, West Virginia, population: two old people and two cats – and a scarecrow."

Grandpa Ed.

GRANDPA ED'S BEDTIME STORIES

OLE PIG

BY JAMES E. MARTIN

PIG

Pig was a pig
Pig was little, because he was not very big
He was a cute little porker with an inquisitive nose
Had a fat little tummy and eight pointed toes
His little brown eyes had a mischievous twinkle
And his turned-up snout caused his eyebrows to wrinkle
He was black on both ends and white in the middle
Had large floppy ears and a curled tail that was little

Gramps built Pig a pen and a neat little house
Where Pig could relax just as snug as a mouse
Pig loved mud above all else except eating
Was untidy in appearance and in his housekeeping
Gramps was dismayed when he saw Pig in mud to his knees
He told Granny, "When winter comes, that pig is going to freeze.
I'll fetch some clean straw to make him a bed
And maybe some gumption will come to his head."

As time passed by, winter winds came squalling
Snow flakes piled up and temperatures kept falling
And Pig's house was a mess as he just stood there
With jello-like shivers shivering beneath his very thin hair
Here is a natural fact that you might want to 'dig'
You'll never find nary a patch of fur on a pig
One would think that when cold winter winds started to blow
Dumb pigs into hibernation would go

Gramps loved that little pig, did not want him to suffer
He would move him into the warm barn one way or another
But how to get him there would be a puzzling chore
A one hundred yard distance from Pig's front door
Another natural fact that you might want to 'dig'
It is almost impossible to drive a pig
But Fate smiled when college Son came home, a holiday to spend
Gramps said, "Son, I need your help down at the pig pen."

The drifts were deep, a blizzard had blown
Almost the worse weather old Gramps had ever known
Together the men opened the gate to the pen
And that is when the fun began
Pig rocketed out and disappeared in a drift of snow
To guess where he went was difficult to know
First there was a glimpse of tail, then a glimpse of snout
The question was where would that pig pop out?

Gramps got ready and had himself all set
When Pig exploded out of that drift like a jet
The old man foresaw an imminent battle
He grabbed Pig's ears and upon his back jumped astraddle
Pig decided that this was a time to play
With a squeal and a snort tried getting away
And where was Son during all of this?
He was rolling on the ground having a laughing fit

Gramps knew that for Pig's safety, he could not let go
For left unprotected, Pig would die in the snow
A misty blur they struggled in mad illusion
What was man and what was pig defined total confusion
But at last a snowman staggered out of that waist deep drift
Clutching a pig that he was barely able to lift

Pig was kicking and walking his four feet in mid-air
Squealing his lungs out with his mouth beside Gramp's right ear

"Please help me Son! This load is too big
I need you to help me carry this dadburned pig!"

It was no time for making lengthy speeches
Old Pig was almost shaking Gramps right out of his britches

Son just held his sides and kept right on laughing
All the while, Old Pig just kept on kicking and squawking
Gramps somehow managed to walk to the barn
While his poor brain was shattered by that one-pig alarm

Ah! The barn at last, Gramps thrust Old Pig through the door
With his heart almost exploding, Gramps fell to the floor
Son clung to the side of a stall still erupting with glee
He said, "That was the funniest thing that I ever did see."
Pig was contentedly grunting while exploring his new bed
While Gramps was trying to clear the ringing noise from his head
There is a Moral to this story you should carefully hear,
If you carry pigs, teach them to whisper and not squeal in
your ear

Written for and presented to Mrs. Polk's 1995 second grade class,
White Sulphur Springs Elementary School, West Virginia

I'M THE FANG

Shortly after little Timmy's fifth birthday, a spinal infection paralyzed both of his legs. No longer would he be able to walk or run when he played. He always loved to romp with his little friends and to run in the park with his Mother, Father, and his little dog Pretzel. Now his visits to the park was by being pushed in a wheelchair or carried upon his Father's shoulders. Pretzel could not understand why his little friend no longer romped with him in the park. At first, Timmy was very sad until one day he saw a little girl who was blind. How terrible it was to be blind, he thought. What must it be like not to be able to see the beauties of the earth, not to see his parent's kind smiling faces, not to see his friends, nor his dog, Pretzel. Everything considered, Timmy believed that he was a very lucky little boy. The main things were that he was otherwise healthy and that he was dearly loved by his parents.

Timmy's father was a fighter pilot in the United States Air Force where he flew an F-16 jet which he nicknamed 'The Fang'. He hired an artist to paint a cartoon picture of a large grey wolf upon each side of the plane's nose cowling. Both Timmy and his father were very fond of "The Fang". Timmy never missed an opportunity to visit 'The Fang' with his father. Many times when his father was flying a training mission and was returning to base, he would fly over their house and would wag 'The Fang's' wings to let Timmy know if was his father flying.

When Timmy became old enough to join, several of his closest friends entered a local Cub Scout Pack. He felt a great sorrow when he thought that he could not be included with his friends because of his condition. He told his parents about his disappointment, but to his surprise, they answered that there was no reason why he could not become a Cub Scout, if he wanted to. His father was an Eagle Scout during his youth, so he would gladly help young Timmy become a Cub Scout. What was equally exciting, Timmy's mother also volunteered to become the Pack's assistant Den Mother. That way, she could not only help with the Pack's training activities, but she would always be present to help Timmy with his wheelchair.

Being a member of the Cub Scouts was great fun for Timmy. The lessons that Scouting taught about clean living, honesty, truthfulness, loyalty, self reliance, and love of mankind and one's country made Timmy happy that he was alive. He enjoyed the cookouts, the fellowship of his den mates, and the lessons he learned about accomplishing things with his hands and his mind. He realized that he would never be able to fly an Air Force jet like his father, but he was certain that, with the help of his loving parents, there would be a rewarding life awaiting him if he prepared himself.

Sometimes, life's events take a drastic and unexpected turn that is difficult to understand. Such had been the case when Timmy's legs became useless. Fate was not quite finished with Timmy's legs, however. His parents had never given up hope that by some miracle, he would get well and be able to walk again. Little did they know that he would actually be able to walk again, but not just quite the way in which they had been hoping. In spite of having Timmy attended by the finest doctors and hospitals in the Nation, the use of his legs could not be restored.

A crisis gradually developed, very slowly at first and then an emergency. You see, the lack of exercise and the poor circulation in Timmy's withered legs reached the point where the doctors told Timmy and his parents that both of his legs would have to be amputated to save his life. Although Timmy faced that news bravely, conclucing that his legs were useless to him anyway, his parents, on the other hand, were greatly distressed.

Timmy told his parents that he had two requests before he went to the hospital. The first was that he wanted his father to take him back to the air base to see 'The Fang' one more time. The other involved an event which Timmy had heard announced on television about a large number of eighteen wheel truck drivers who were planning to spend a weekend at the local fairground conducting a Child Wish. A Child Wish is an event at which handicapped children and those who are extremely ill are granted their fondest wish. Many children, including Timmy, loved to see big fancy road rigs. Once each year, the truck drivers select a city where they invite children to visit with them and examine their trucks. They take kids for slow rides around the race track, give them gifts, and treat them to refreshments. They donate caps, belt buckles, company patches, and key chains. Many of them furnish the children with their radio call name, or 'handle'. There are as many 'handles' as there are truck drivers. There are such names as Lonesome George, Rambling Wreck, Barefoot Sam, Rough Ralph, Poor Boy, and many others.

Timmy's parents were pleased to grant his request. First, Timmy's father got special permission from Base Security to allow him to take

Timmy down the flight line where the squadron's F-16s were parked. Timmy was amazed by the awesome sight as they drove past dozens of planes until finally they arrived where 'The Fang' was parked. Timmy was even more amazed when he saw the painting of the big gray wolf.

His father had the artist to repaint it so that now the wolf was wearing a dark blue Cub Scout uniform complete with a cap and a yellow scarf! What was more, 'The Fang' was wearing Timmy's Pack number on his shoulder. Timmy was overcome with joy.

The next day, Timmy's parents took him to Child Wish. There were hundreds of trucks of every size, color, and type. There were also hundreds of kids. Truck drivers, both men and women, many of them husband and wife teams, many with their family dogs or cats, all gave the children a hearty welcome. Once more, Timmy was overjoyed. He was given several rides, he blew air horns, stepped on brake pedals which made the sound of escaping air, he collected many badges and pins, some patches, and a bright red cap. He was allowed to talk on a CB radio to some of the drivers in other trucks parked at the fairground. One driver asked him, "What is your 'handle' partner?" Timmy told him proudly, "I'm The Fang."

Well, the day came when Timmy went to the hospital for his surgery. It took great courage for a small boy to have both legs amputated, but the surgery was a success in that it saved his life. He spent many weeks recovering, but, as Timmy's father could tell him from first hand experience in flying 'The Fang', clouds really do have a 'silver living'. With Timmy's useless legs out of the way, he was fitted with the most modern artificial legs. With them being able to support his weight through the use of crutches, it was no longer necessary for Timmy to be confined to a wheelchair. After a few weeks of training, he could walk once more unassisted! But Timmy did not stop there. He entered special training, and within months, he learned how to walk again without the crutches. He could not run, but by golly, he could walk!

Now it is time to go 'fast forward' several years. Timmy grew to become a handsome young man. He attended the finest university of aeronautical engineering. Shortly after graduation, his father retired from the Air Force. Together, they opened a flight school. Not only did they teach other young people how to fly, but Timmy's father also taught Timmy how to fly. His personal plane was not a F-16, but Timmy was now the owner and pilot of a sleet Lear Jet, which of course he named 'TheFang'.

James E. Martin

TOLIVER TURNIP

To the people of Bumpus Mill, Toliver Turnip was a strange name for a man. It was, in fact, a strange name for a strange man. When he arrived in the sleepy dusty little country village of Bumpus Mill just before sundown one warm summer afternoon riding a decrepit flea bitten old nag named Stagger and leading an equally scroungy old pack mule whom he called Corpse, the three of them looked as though they were rejects from a rubbish land fill.

They could not avoid attracting attention, not that they arrived in the village like a storm, but just the opposite. The animals moved so slowly that one would expect that their next step would be their last. No doubt, if they had reached Bumpus Mill after dark, and if the cargo that the animals were carrying had not made a clattering sound with each step, they may have passed through the village with its single unpaved and unlighted street completely unnoticed.

It was difficult to tell if Toliver Turnip was even awake, viewing him from the side, he looked very much like a very thin cardboard cut-out of a hatchet-faced scare crow. His posture was so poor that his body curved in the shape of a question mark as he slumped in the saddle atop Old Stagger. Tolliver Turnip was very tall and skinny. His pole shaped body appeared to be the same size around from the ankles above his enormous feet to his corn cob shaped neck. His face was so narrow that his steel blue eyes almost came together. They were prevented from doing so by his thin high-bridged hawk-bill shaped nose positioned above a small mouth and almost no chin, thus giving him the facial features of an eagle. A long handlebar style mustache with pointed ends reached beyond the middle of his face on each side. The weight of a tall black pointed hay stack shaped hat much like those seen in pictures of Halloween witches seemed to rest entirely upon his bent down ears and upon his great black bushy eyebrows. To say it simply Toliver Turnip was a very strange looking man.

Old Stagger was also a sight to behold. When viewed from the side, he looked more like a child's wooden play horse than a real one. If you can imagine a large wooden mallet with a handle, then you have an image of Old Stagger's head and neck. He had a long head that resembled a block of wood with a long clump of hair growing from between two small

84

pointed ears. The hair hung over the front of his brow and completely hid his eyes. The area around his nose was covered by long fuzzy white down-like hair which looked like some old man's flowing beard. His relaxed lower lip was so thick and heavy that it dangled limply exposing his aging large yellow teeth.

Where the necks of most horses are arched on top, Old Stagger's sagged in the middle like an upturned piece of watermelon rind. His shoulders were so bony at the point where his neck joined, they resembled twin hill tops. His back sagged in the middle just as his neck did, seeming to force everything downward into his bulging pot belly. The two peaks forming his hip bones matched those of his shoulders.

Besides Toliver Turnip and the saddle, Old Stagger carried a large bed roll and a large assortment of pots, pans, ladles, skillets, and buckets dangling from cords tied to every available space around the edge of the saddle. The heavy load carried by that ancient horse caused his four legs to sprawl outward as he struggled to keep his balance. Toliver Turnip allowed the reins to dangle limply as Old Stagger stumbled along the dusty road, his eyes drooping almost asleep, and his nose almost touching the ground. With each step, the pots and pans made a merry clattering sound.

Old Corpse, the pack mule, trailed along behind, being lead by a long rope tied to a ring on the back of Old Stagger's saddle. The mule was a good match for Stagger, except that the mule had a much better shape. Judging from the long snow white hair which grew around his eyes, from the insides of his long ears, around his nose, and beneath his belly, the mule must have been very old. He carried a wooden pack saddle and the bulging load covered by a large sheet of canvas gave him the shape of a very large football. The canvas and the load beneath it was held in place by long ropes which crisscrossed the bundle. In addition to more pots and pans, picks and shovels were tucked under the ropes of his pack.

It was obvious to a trained eye, the old geezer, Toliver Turnip was a gold prospector. He had come down from the high mountains and deep canyons to buy food for himself and feed for his animals. The animals were carrying everything that Toliver Turnip owned. By living the way that he did, he was at home no matter where he was.

The old man was a strange sight, even in the remote country village of Bumpus Mill. As they entered the edge of the village, the clatter and the tingle of the pots and pans attracted the attention of several neighborhood dogs who began to bark loudly as they followed the slow progress of the travelers. The commotion became so noisy that startled cats scampered into hiding.

Little children also began to follow the trio's slow progress on the way to Bumpus Mill's only watering trough, which was located in front of Bumpus Mill's only general store. Toliver Turnip dismounted from Old Stagger and tied the animals to the hitching posts located beside the watering trough. Even his spurs made a merry jingling sound as he walked across the wooden porch and entered the store.

By that time, most of the people who lived at Bumpus Mill had gathered at the store to gaze at the strange travelers. They crowded inside the store's front door and upon the porch so that they could hear the conversation between Tolvier Turnip and Mr. Friendly, the merchant.

"Howdy Stranger", said Mr. Friendly.

"Howdy. The name is Toliver Turnip", replied Toliver.

"Where are you from? Asked Mr. Friendly.

"No place in particular", answered Toliver Turnip.

"How may I help you?" asked Mr. Friendly.

Toliver Turnip removed a leather pouch which was closed by a draw string from his pocket. He dumped the contents upon the top of the counter and said, "I would like to trade you some of these gold nuggets for some supplies," he said.

Mr. Friendly said, "I'll be pleased to furnish you whatever you want."

"I need some flour, salt, sugar, coffee, pepper, bacon, lard, matches, and a couple twists of chawing tobaccie," said Toliver Turnip. "I also need some oats and shelled corn fer my animals," he continued.

Mr. Friendly gathered all of the supplies which Toliver Turnip ordered and said, "Well, that is everything you ordered. Did you also need a few bars of soap?"

"Nope," responded Tolvier Turnip. "I never touch the stuff."

Mr. Friendly helped Toliver Turnip carry his supplies out to where Old Stagger and Corpse were waiting. Toliver Turnip loaded most of it onto poor Old Corpse and mounted Old Stagger to leave.

"Where are you going?" asked Mr. Friendly.

"No place in particular," answered Toliver Turnip as he began riding away clattering down the road into the gathering darkness and slowly rattled out of sight.

The barking dogs who had greeted the travelers upon their arrival were now escorting them out of the village. Some of them were having fun nipping at Old Corpse's heels, causing him to skitter nervously from one side of the narrow road to the other. One by one, the dogs gave up the chase and returned to their homes.

That was all except one, a coon hound pup named Chigger. Young Chigger was caught up in all of the excitement. In fact, that was the most excitement that Chigger had ever experienced. It made him feel good to get out of the yard and to run on the street with the big dogs. Besides that, Chigger enjoyed following down wind from that mangy mule and horse, inhaling the heavy aroma that their sweaty bodies left lingering on the summertime evening air. He also enjoyed the tinkling sounds made by the pots and pans. Instead of turning back with the other dogs, Young Chigger decided that he wanted to leave home and join Toliver Turnip in his travels. He wanted to live the life of a prospector's pup, to spend his life in the freedom of the high peaks and deep canyons of the Great Rocky Mountains.

Toliver Turnip sat in stony silence staring straight ahead. He was not aware that Chigger pup was quietly trotting along beside Old Corpse. Chigger, himself, was amusing to watch as he trotted along in that awkward zig zagging clumbsy manner of a growing pup whose feet seem to be too large and whose tall upright tail seems so heavy that in wags the pup's hips off balance.

Toliver Turnip only became aware that Chigger had joined his party when a rabbit became alarmed by the clattering of the pots and pans. The rabbit scampered up the road darting quickly to one side of the road and then the other before finally disappearing beneath a clump of tall weeds and bushes. Chigger could not resist exploding into a clopping gallop as he chased the rabbit. The clumbsy pup was no match for the swift nimble rabbit, so he soon gave up the chase.

Realizing that Toliver Turnip now knew his secret, Chigger returned to face him. He looked sheepishly up at the tall man in the saddle. He pleaded with his soft brown eyes and softly whimpered as though asking for acceptance. Toliver Turnip had reined Old Stagger to a halt as he stared with icy sternness at the skinny pup.

"Where are you going, Chigger?" asked Toliver Turnip.

"No where in particular," answered Chigger.

"Well, don't you reckon we had better be getting started?" answered Toliver Turnip.

With Country Love,
Grandpa Ed

GRANDPA ED'S BEDTIME STORIES

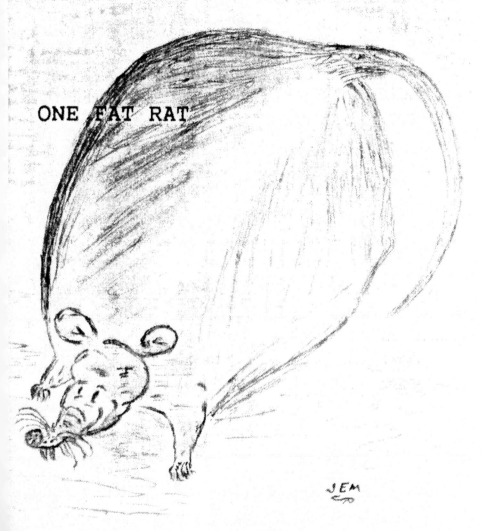

ONE FAT RAT

BY JAMES E. MARTIN

James E. Martin

ONE FAT RAT

Once there was a young rat who lived in a very poor run-down neighborhood on the edge of a large city. His parents were poor and he had so many brothers and sisters that there never was enough food to eat. He was hungry most of the time. As did most rats of the world who lived inside mines, in the hulls of ships, or near filthy garbage dumps, Rat and his family scrounged about in trash dumpsters and filthy back alleys to hunt scraps of food. Most of what they did find did not taste good. Sometimes what he did eat also made him sick. There were times when he ate spoiled fruit which had fermented into alcohol made him drunk causing him to sleep for an entire day at a time.

As though that was not bad enough, Rat and his family were not very well liked by others living in their neighborhood, especially by people. There were also many ferocious alley cats who were also very hungry and thought of rats as their next meal. For that reason, Rat had to become an expert at watching his back, never making himself a target for cats who could move as fast as lightning. He also had to learn that his body was not safely hidden if he forgot to pull his long tail into his hiding place. If a cat spied his tail sticking out unprotected, the cat could pull him out of his hiding place and eat him. That happened to him once when he just barely escaped that awful cat's clutches, but his poor tail was painfully wounded. Weeks passed before the pain went away, but the long scars still remain to this very day.

One bright sunny morning, something very exciting, but also very scary, began happening in Rat's neighborhood. A group of men wearing yellow hard hats brought very noisy huge machines and began knocking down all of the buildings to clean a ten acre vacant lot. Bulldozers, dump trucks, ditch diggers, road graders, tar spreaders, cement mixers, and cranes were everywhere. Great flood light were mounted on tall poles lighting the area so that the terrible noise continued both day and night. It was frightening enough to cause a poor rat's nerves to jangle! What was worse, there were ten acres less places to find food. Now all of the cat and rat population were crowded into the alleys remaining in the community. More crowded cats meant more danger. More rats crowded into a smaller area where food was already scarce caused many bad tempers and fights. Rat made up his mind that he was not going to live under those conditions.

It soon became apparent that the men were building a large warehouse with many truck docks and a vast paved parking lot. Some men were busy spreading and rolling the asphalt smooth, while others were busy using paint machines to stripe hundreds of parking spaces. Others used lift platforms to install lights and wires atop tall lamp posts. Fork lifts scampered about in all directions carrying pallets of blocks, lumber, and roofing to the carpenters and masons who were building the huge warehouse.

Rat quietly crept beneath the construction office trailer where he could overhear what was being planned. That was how he learned that the warehouse was going to become the main supply point for a large grocery company. He heard the foreman say, "This is going to be the most modern warehouse anywhere. One thing for certain, I want it to be rat-proof! There won't be a hole left anywhere bigger than a key hole! Now see to it."

That was not welcome news to Rat. All of that wonderful food was going to be plopped down right in the middle of his neighborhood and he would not be able to get even a bit of it. He thought not, so be began making plans to get inside that building while it was being built. He saw his chance when a fork lift went over to the edge of the big parking lot to pick up a load of insulation. Rat hid inside the open space in the end of one of the rolls. Once inside the building, all that he had to do was remain quietly out of sight. There were so many men and fork lifts scurrying about helter skelter, it certainly was no place for a rat to leave his tail sticking out. Rat knew that he was going to find plenty of food to eat while the building was being constructed, because careless workers left scraps of their lunches lying about in paper bags. In fact, their scraps were some of the finest food which Rat had ever eaten. Now all that he had to do was to stay well hidden and allow the rat-proof building to be closed up around him. If he stayed alert, he would be set for life. He knew that his survival depended upon him never being seen. His secret must be kept forever.

Within a few weeks, Rat was surrounded by tons upon tons of every kind of food imaginable. During his earlier life, he almost wore his teeth out gnawing through walls and digging into tough plastic garbage bags just to reach food. Now he had only to sneak out of any one of thousands of hiding places at night to eat the finest of fruits, vegetables, and nuts. Rat knew that he must be the most lucky rat on earth. He avoided poison rat bait that was placed at various places throughout the warehouse. He did not have to eat anything that he did not want.

There was one very great problem, however. Rat was becoming so fat that he was in danger of bursting. He was becoming so fat that he had great difficulty walking. Running was something that he could no longer do. He was becoming so heavy that his legs could barely carry his body. If there was danger, he feared that he could not move fast enough to save himself. He was now almost as broad as he was long! He was one very fat rat.

Rat's eyes stayed the same size, but they were almost puffed shut by fat. His ears were still the same size, but they were pushed so high upon his head that his scalp was about to split. His nose was the same size, but it was almost hid by his puffy jaws. His feet were the same size they had always been, but his body was so fat that he could no longer see his feet. His tail was the same size as always, but Rat was so fat that he could not bend his neck far enough to see the tip of it.

Just as Rat was in the process of exploding like an overly inflated balloon, Bobby awakened from his dreamy nap at his school room desk. His teacher and all of his classmates were laughing at him because he had dozed and had almost fallen off his chair.

"Are you still with us, Bobby?" his teacher asked while the other children giggled.

"Oh, I have the most interesting story to tell you. Once there was a young rat who lived in a very poor run-down neighborhood...," he began.

Just at the very moment, a bell rang ending the school day. Bobby was left standing in mid-sentence as all of his classmates rushed from the room to catch school buses which would take them home.

"Grandpa Ed"

AUTUMN'S DROOPY DONKEY

Droopy was a sad little donkey. He was sad mostly because he was so tiny. He was tiny because he was a miniture donkey. Miniture donkeys do not grow up to be big donkeys. Droopy thought that because he was so little, compared to the large farm animals, that he was useless. What Droopy did not realize was that he was not the smallest creature on the farm. He was much larger than a bug, a bee, or a bird. He was also bigger than a cat, a lamb, or even the farm dog. He was larger than a mouse, a rabbit, or a possum. He legs were longer, his body was longer, he weighed more, his tail was longer, and his ears were longer than any of them. Besides, Droopy was a beautiful little animal.

Poor Droopy. He was so unhappy and his mind was full of doubt. Doubt was something that he had a lot of. He was getting into a very bad way. He was burning himself up inside with doubt and self-pity. He began to doubt that daylight would ever come again when night time came. Then he would doubt that night time would ever come again after the sun rose in the morning. He doubted that the sun would ever shine again after a rain. He didn't think that little flowers planted in pots on the farm house porch would grow to be big flowers. He didn't think that anything young or little such as baby birds, kittens, pups, or piglets would grow big, because he was little. Besides, he was even sadder because he did not think that he had a friend in the whole world.

Droopy lived in dread of every day. He did not run and play, even when the other young farm creatures such as the frisky calves, the piglets, the lambs, and the collie puppies invited him to romp with them. Droopy just hid himself from view inside the darkest part of the big barn. After a while, the other animals just quit trying to be his friend. He was no fun to be around, so they just left him alone.

One warm day in early June when schools had closed for the summer, the people who owned the farm were greatly excited. Little Autumn, who lived in the big city of White Sulphur Springs and had never visited a farm, was coming to spend the summer with her Aunt Millie and Uncle Mort. They had bought this farm which had a large comfortable house surrounded by a shady lawn, many farm buildings, and hundreds of acres of fields. It was truly one of the world's beauty spots. Aunt Millie and

Uncle Mort did not have any children, so little Autumn brought them great joy by just coming to stay at their house.

Aunt Millie's house was so large that Autumn spent one entire day just exploring it. There was the great entrance hallway, the large living room, the parlor, the dining room with crystal chandlier, the second floor bed rooms atop the winding stairway. And ah! The attic filled with so many keepsake treasures! There were many dark closets and the big basement which smelled like a cave. The porch with its white banisters and lovely potted flowers wrapped around three sides of the great house. Autumn's favorite room inside the farm house was Aunt Millie's spicy smelling great kitchen where she cooked some of the best food in the world.

The next day, Autumn went outside to explore the many buildings which created the barn yard. Some were small buildings such as the smoke house, the wood shed, pump house, and hen house. She was amazed at the large machine shed where many kinds of farm equipment was stored. She said, "Wow!" when she saw the huge tractors and the grain combine which was as big as a two-car garage. Autumn then strolled beyond the machine shed to where the great barn was located. The crest of its roof must have been fifty feet above the ground, its aluminum cover gleaming in the bright sunlight. Near one end of the barn stood three giant sized silos, each of which stood sixty feet tall. Their rounded aluminum noses also gleamed as they stood there like huge missiles awaiting to be launched into outer space.

Autumn felt like she was only a tiny dot as she entered a large open doorway of the building nearly half the size of a football field. Everywhere she looked, she saw stables and pens and rooms. Families of cattle, horses, and sheep were relaxing inside the barn to shade themselves from the hot sun. Autumn was anxious to see the great hay mow on the second floor. She climbed stairs to reach it. Vast stockpiles of hay were stored at many places about the huge room, but great expanses of open space still remained. Autumn was thinking what a wonderful place for a playhouse this would be.She made plans to spend a lot of time playing there, but she still had some more exploring to do.

She returned to the ground level to make sure that she didn't miss seeing anything of interest. That was when she discovered Droopy hiding himself in a dark corner where he thought nobody would find him. With Autumn, it was love at first sight. Droopy was the cutest animal that she had ever seen.

She said, "Hi there!" "Do you want to play?""

She knelt upon her knees and placed her arms around his neck. She patted him with her hands. She gently stroked his long ears and nose.

Droopy had never seen a girl before. In fact, he had never had anyone to play with before. He didn't know who she was, but he really liked the attention he was getting. She was making him feel important for the very first time in his life. He was pressing against Autumn and was hoping that she would not go away. Actually, Autumn had been wondering after she had made the plan to spend the summer with Aunt Millie and Uncle Mort if she would find anyone to play with during the long summer. Now she knew that she had found a perfect playmate.

Autumn lead Droopy out of the darkness into the more lighted part of the stall. There she saw a brush resting upon a shelf; the kind which stablemen use to groom horses. She took the brush into her hands and began to brush Droopy's fine hair. The more she brushed, the more his hair shined. Autumn spent a half hour giving Droopy a complete grooming. Droopy thought that was the greatest thing which had ever happened to him. His spirits were rising and, for the first time, he began to feel happy. He actually believed that someone loved him. That felt good. What was more, he felt that he was important. Autumn noticed a trunk-like wooden box with a hinged lid positioned near Droopy's stall. She raised the lid and discovered that it was full of sweet feed for horses. It looked almost like granola and smelled almost good enough for her to eat. She gathered a hand full and held it near Droopy's mouth. Droopy immediately began eating the sweet feed out of Autumn's hand. Autumn giggled because his fuzzy nose tickled her hand as he ate.

She began to run circles inside the stall to see if Droopy would follow her. At first, Droopy did not seem to know how to play. You see, he hadn't had much practice at playing, so it seemed a little strange to stop feeling sorry for himself long enough to have some fun. But he realized that this little girl, his newly found friend, wanted him to play with her, so, before long, he began chasing her around the stable. He had never had fun before, but he soon learned that it felt good and he liked it. Soon, Autumn opened the stable gate and she and Droopy ran out into the sunlight and the huge barnyard. First he chased her and then she chased him.

The two new friends played hard the rest of the afternoon. Finally they became tired. Autumn gathered Droopy a hand full of sweet clover to eat. She sat down and leaned her back against the base of a large elm tree. Droopy lay with his head resting on her lap as he munched the clover. Soon they were sound asleep. That was where Uncle Mort and his farm helpers found them when they returned from the fields at the end of the day.

"I see you found Droopy," said Uncle Mort as he gently shook Autumn's shoulder to awaken her.

"I didn't know his name," Autumn murmered as she looked up at her Uncle's smiling face through sleepy eyes, "But we had lots of fun" she continued.

"Well, you can feed him his supper and give him a drink of water," said Uncle Mort, "and then you had better come to the house. Your Aunt Millie will be wondering what has happened to you."

From that day onward, Autumn and Droopy were the best of friends. They spent every day together. They played in the barn, they played on the lawn, they roamed the huge fields, and sometimes visited Uncle Mort where he was doing the farm work with his helpers. Sometimes Aunt Millie would use one of the farm trucks to carry lunch and cool drinks out to Uncle Mort and his helpers in the large fields. Autumn and Droopy would sit upon the floor of the truck bed to ride out with her. The way Aunt Millie would serve lunch from the tailgate of the truck was like having a picnic with sanwiches, fruit, pie, and lemonade. There always was sweet clover for Droopy to nibble if he was hungry.

One night before bedtime, Autumn said to Aunt Millie and Uncle Mort, "May I please change the little donkey's name from Droopy to Happy?"

"Ofcourse you can," they both answered at the same time, "Why do you ask?"

"Well, you see, he is such a happy little animal and Droopy just does not fit him very well," Autumn answered.

"I think Happy would be a very fitting name for your little friend," said Aunt Millie as she gave Autumn a loving hug.

"Your little friend is right," added Uncle Mort, "For you see, we are going to give him to you to take home as your very own at the end of the summer. We have already cleared it with your folks. "

"Yip-e-e!," shouted Autumn. Now I don't know which one you should name Happy."

"I think that we can get along with two," said kindly Uncle Mort.

CHARITY EMMALINA REBECCA BELL McNAB McVEE

Charity Emmalina Rebecca Bell McNab McVee was a lady just as prim and proper as she could be, a daughter of the Alde Sod of Ireland across the broad Atlantic Sea. At one's first glance, she looked like the 'nanny' sort; ramrod straight, but neither tall nor short. Although filled with goodness within, she almost never showed a smile nor a grin. Her appearance was tidy, na a hair outta place, no lipstick or powder or paint on her face. She wore white gloves and a hat held on with a pin and a kerchief across the top and tied under her chin. An umbrella hooked on the crook of her arm; a purse held in her hand to keep her belongings safe from harm.

To America she came aboard a very big ship at a time when winter's cold gives one's nose a sharp nip. It made her cheeks turn rosy and she wrapped in a shawl to keep out the shivers when the snow blew in squalls. Down the gangplank she came with her heels making clicks and her arms and her legs keeping time like two busy drum sticks.

To become a 'School Marm' McVee wanted to be, so twas direct to a 'Master' she went to see. She said, "I love lassies and ladies of every kind and Aye want to teach them how to improve their young minds."

So there she stands daily behind her desk, as stern as a judge as she performs her task, but the Kiddies all love her because she is really a jewel. To make fun of her looks would be most unkind and cruel, for that sort of behavior is a real 'no-no' you know and finding fault with others is an act that should go.

So instead of stories about Dick and Jane, McVee told Irish stories about O'Patrick and Shane. But children are really much alike the whole world around. The greatest difference are the customs in their homes where they are found. The games which they play are much the same, just different Lands with different names.

And so it was in Lady McVee's classroom where much larnin' took place and all hearts were in tune. From the simplest One plus Two makes Three to how Christopher Columbus made world history. She told of a little Dutch boy who, upon one awful night, plugged a hole in the dike with his fist saving his village from flood and a terrible plight. Also a sea story about ship wrecks upon Inescape Rock and of a kind old merchant

97

who hung a bell upon its top so sailors could hear it ring when in storms their ships were tossed. Then they could steer to a safer way and live to sail again another day. The story went on to tell how an evil pirate captain had his renegade crew remove that bell! Then one awesome night his own ship was being tossed upon the darkened sea and he did not know where the dreaded Inescape Rock could be. But his ship found the rock all by itself as the pirates cringed with the terrible fear that they felt. All hands were lost except one who lived to tell how the Pirate Captain prayed that he could hear that bell.

McVee used such stories to teach that one's deeds should always be good, although you may be by others misunderstood.

She was a shining light for all to see, that Charity Emmalina Rebecca Bell McNab McVee. Parents brought their children from miles around to see this living Saint whom they had accidently found; that gracious Lady from so far away who had come to their little town to stay. Hundreds of children during thirty five years passed through her class remembering how as a wee lad or tiny lass, they learned good citizens to be while also learning their ABCs.

Long after the children were grown and gone to work at jobs and raise families of their own, they would return to their old School Marm to see the kind, the gentle, the saintly McVee. They recall those happy days of long ago, those carefree times when life was slow, when their Mommies and Daddys tucked them into bed and stories were told just before prayers were said. "Please protect Mommy, Daddy, Sister, Brother, and me and kindly remember our dear School Teacher, Miss McNab McVee."

So alas! came the time when McVee's life was gone and the town's folk built a statue of her upon the school house lawn. It was carved from pure white stone with marble slabs to rest upon. Inscribed with bold letters for all to see were the words, 'In Loving Memory Of Our Greatest Teacher, Charity Emmalina Rebecca Bell McNab McVee.

O'SHAUNASEE MAC'DOULE

One bright summer day, Timmy and his older brother Shane were at a high mountain park having a picnic with their parents and a large group of their neighbors. The picnic area was surrounded by a very large forest. There were many children who were free to run and play anywhere within the picnic grounds, just as long as they did not stray into the forest.

The picnic area had swings, slides, a trampoline tent, monkey bars, a large long black tube to crawl through, seesaws, an exercise trail, and a stream to wade in. There were also long tables loaded with many kinds of good food including wonderful desserts, ice-cream, and watermellon.

A large number of children were playing a game of hide-and-seek. Timmy wanted to join them and he asked Shane to help him find a good place to hide. Together, they ran into the edge of the forest where they entered a tangled thicket of rhododendron. What a great place to hide! Nobody would ever find them there. Well, a baby deer thought it was a great place to hide also. That cute little critter must have been only a few hours old, because his little legs wobbled when he arose to his feet when the little boys frightened him. He began to run as well as he could deeper into the thicket searching for his mother. Timmy and Shane were so excited, they could not resist following the little deer. They could not run very fast through the tangled undergrowth. For a short time, the boys kept the little animal in sight, but the fawn could slip through the tangled limbs easier than the boys could. Soon they could no longer see him.

It was then that they knew that they had made a big mistake. Beneath the Rhododendron's thick overhead canopy, the sun could not be seen. The eerie gloom seemed like the coming of night. The boys did not know how far they had traveled and they lost all sense of direction, because the thicket looked exactly the same in all directions. They had left no tracks upon the forest's leafy floor, so there was no way to retrace their steps. Neither had ever been alone in a forest before and now they were lost and nobody knew where they were. It would not be many hours before the arrival of darkness. What were they to do?

Timmy began to cry and he said, "Shane, I'm scared and I want Mommy!"

Shane realized that he must be brave, so he forced back his own tears. He took Timmy by his hand and they began walking away from where they last saw the baby deer, but Shane soon knew that he could not walk in a straight line inside the tangled thicket. He also knew that they must keep walking if they ever hoped to find their way back to the picnic area. All the while, Timmy kept crying and saying that he was tired and hungry.

After what seemed like hours of painful scratches and aching muscles, the thicket ended and now the two boys entered a giant forest. Shane reasoned that if he walked around the thicket, they would return to the the picnic area. That was a good idea, but the thicket was so broad they could not walk around it. After what seemed like miles, the thicket entered a very steep hollow and the boys found themselves walking down a mountain side. Shane remembered that someone had told him, if you are lost and you keep walking downhill, you will eventually come to where someone lives in a valley. People there can help you get home.

Long before reaching this point, Timmy had grown much too tired to walk, so Shane had been carrying his little brother piggy-back fashion. Although Shane was also growing very tired, he knew that he had to keep going. He thought that it was much too dangerous to follow the edge of the thicket into the deep hollow. He could clearly see the sun now. It was sinking low above a distant ridge, so at least he now knew which direction was West. He decided to travel the ridge-line upon which he stood and follow the direction of the sun. That was a lucky move, for he had walked only a short distance before he discovered a well traveled trail slicing across the ridge and leading around the side of the mountain toward the West! Timmy was still quietly crying, but Shane's heart began pounding with excitement.

He said, "Timmy, We are going to be found! This trail will lead us to safety, but we must hurry. Night time will come soon and we must be out of these woods before dark."

After a few more steps he said, "Timmy, I am very tired and I need to rest. The trail is so steep, I may fall with you on my back and hurt both of us. It is easy to walk down hill, so you must walk for a while. I'm tired. To make it easier for you, I will let you walk in front so you can set your own pace."

The two brothers did not feel so scared now that they had found the trail. Almost at once, they began seeing human shoe tracks and both bicycle and horse tracks. They felt sure that it would not be long before they would find someone to help them. The hour was getting late and now the sun was mostly hidden behind a tall mountain peak. Timmy was becoming frightened once more when an owl began trumpeting whoo!

whoo! whoo! announcing the coming of night. Shane paused long enough to give little brother a comforting hug.

"Shane, I am really scared," said Timmy, who began crying once more.

"Be brave a little while longer, Timmy," replied Shane, trying to sound confident. "We will find help soon. I know we will. Just wait, you'll see. The trail is not so steep now. I'll carry you again for a while."

Help came sooner than they expected when they heard a man singing with a loud voice. "On the bonny banks, upon the bonny banks where the sun shines bright on the glowmin, me and me true love may never meet again on the bonny banks of Locke Lomond."

The two small boys came into view of the man around a bend of the trail just as he was ending his song and was sticking a huge broad axe into the trunk of a tree, which had fallen beside the path. The man was in the act of sitting upon the tree to rest when he caught sight of Shane and Timmy.

"Aye! Bejabers!" boomed the stranger. "Whut d'we ave ere? Two wee ladies it is und aye ney seen two who looks so lost."

He beckoned with his hand, "Come. Come," he said with a friendly voice. "O'Shaunasee Mac'MacDoule aye am. Sit yerself down on this tree a bit an tell me ow aye ken be of service to ya Laddies."

The little boys had never seen such a huge man. He was as big as a giant! Timmy was afraid of him at first, but both boys soon learned that they had nothing to fear from O'Shaunasee Mac'Doule. He must have weighed more than three hundred pounds. He wore a shirt of red and black plaid, blue bibbed overalls, a bright red bandanna handkerchief tied around his neck, and his shoes were almost as long as Timmy was tall. His thick curly hair was colored a mixture of yellow and brown. His deep-set blue eyes sparkled like clear ice as they seemed to dance beneath great bushy eyebrows. His broad jovial face was colored pink and tan like the crinkled surface of a freshly baked plum pudding. His wide toothy grin upon his handsome face was radiant like the Kansas sun rising on a clear summer morning.

As all three sat down upon the fallen tree, the big man said, "So tis lost ye are. Now tell old O'Shaunasee all about it then we'll make plans t'get ye unlost."

"Yes Sir." Responded Shane. "I am Shane Glover and this is my brother, Timmy. We were picnicking with our parents when we followed a baby deer . .," Shane began to say.

"A baby deer t'was," said O'Shaunasee. "Aye can understand that. What about yer folks? They must be worried stiff, ya know."

"Please! Will you help us?" asked Shane.

"Aye, aye Laddie. Aye most certainly will," replied O'Shaunasee. "First, lets get ya outta these dark woods. Aye ave a telephone in me cabin. There must be a search party hunting fer ya now, so I'll call the local police after which Old O'Shaunasee will fix us a bite to eat while we wait for your folks to come and get ya."

So O'Shaunasee picked up his broad axe and the huge man and the tiny boys walked down the trail into the gathering darkness.

"You know how we happened to be in the woods, how did it happen that you were in the woods too, Mr. Mac'Doule?" asked Shane.

"Ah Laddie, ain't ya kind to ask?" answered their new friend. "Ya see, Aye live in the woods, for Ayme a timber cutter ya know. Aye live in a little log cabin with me fat cat Bertha next to the Greenbrier State Forest at Hart Run."

After a short while, O'Shaunasee's log cabin came dimly into view. Bertha seemed to appear out of nowhere as she came to meet the travelers, wiggling her tail and purring loudly. O'Shaunasee lay his axe beside a wood-pile. He stooped down and swept fat Bertha off her feet and cuddled her in his huge arms which were covered with a mass of hair the color and almost the thickness of a grizzly bear's pelt. "Ow ayre ya doin ya little varmit?" O'Shaunasee greeted his little furry friend.

Soon O'Shaunasee and his two visitors entered the snug log cabin. The inside air smelled of a mixture of food, wood smoke, cedar, and pine. The rustic furniture as well as the cabin had the appearance of having been made by O'Shaunasee, himself.

O'Shaunasee said, "Rest ye bones, Laddies, whilst Aye make that most important telephone call, then Aye'll roust up some vittles after which we'll eat and wait."

Having said that, he dialed a number and spoke, "It is O'Shaunasee Mac'Doule Aye am. Aye am reporting that two wee ones av found me out in the high woods; tis Shane and Timmy they are. Quite lost ya know. Their father George Glover it is. The laddiees want that ya call their folks to let them know they are safe."

After he listened to someone who had answered the telephone, O'Shaunasee spoke again, "Aye, that is right. It is by the North edge of The Greenbrier State Forest in me log cabin Aye live. Aye'll fix em some supper and we'll wait for their parents to arrive. Goodbye."

When O'Shaunasee turned around , to tell Shane and Timmy the good news, he saw the two little boys and fat Bertha cuddled together sleeping upon a bear skin rug on the floor in front of the hearth of the open fireplace. The big man stroked his chin with one of his large rough hands and mumbled "bejambers!" And all was well.

James E. Martin

RICO SHAY
RABBIT

RICO SHAY RABBIT

Rico Shay Rabbit and Benny Beagle were born several miles apart on the same day. On that day, they each had much the same thing on their minds. They were just learning to breathe, they were trying to open their eyes, and they were hungry all the time.

Rico Shay had to wait two weeks for his eyes to open so he could see his own fur, see his Mother, and his three sisters, Flossie, Bunny, and Flo.

That Rico Shay was one frisky rabbit. He just could not be still. Even when he was asleep, he twitched and kicked with his feet. It was so bad, his three sisters could not sleep in the same nest with him. Since there were three of them and only one of him, they made him sleep outside the nest. That was not so bad, for when bunnies are born during the springtime, the nights are warm. Having to sleep outside the nest suited Rico Shay just fine. He didn't have to listen to his complaining sisters and he could sleep any way he liked.

Rico Shay Rabbit grew so fast that in no time at all, he was twice as big as each of his sisters. Maybe that was because Rico Shay spent most of his time eating huge bites of clover, carrots, and cabbage.

There was something else that Rico Shay Rabbit loved to do; he loved to run. He would run for no other reason than just for the joy of it. He would race with anyone who would run with him. He would race Cory Colt, Taffy Calf, or Baa Baa Lamb. He even tried to race with birds when they flew across an open field. There were times when Rico Shay tried to outrun his shadow. He was getting good at that racing thing. One that he enjoyed most was racing with butterflies. He would run beneath their flight paths, dart when they darted, turn when they turned, stop when they stopped. That is how he became skilled at making quick, sharp changes in direction at blazing speed. He could turn back to where he came from at almost full speed.

Rico Shay was so proud of his skill, he invited his sisters to practice with him, but they were only interested in staying close to their Mother doing girl things. It was fun to outrun the colt, the calf, and the lambs, but they were not interested in zig zag running. Besides they were too clumsy to even try.

Rico Shay Rabbit was becoming bored with staying close to home, so he began traveling farther and farther away. After a time, he never went home or saw his family at all. He just wandered where ever he pleased.

One day, he discovered Farmer Friendly's ten acre cabbage patch. With all of those acres of food, Rico Shay was sure that he had discovered rabbit heaven. Well, he just hopped right into the field and made himself at home. Not only could he eat all of his favorite food he wanted, he now had a ten acre race course where he could run zig zag among thousands of cabbage heads. Also there were thousands of little white cabbage butterflies to race with.

One day when Rico Shay came racing around the end of a cabbage row, he became face to face, almost nose to nose with Benny Beagle! Rico Shay did not know it, but Benny Beagle was born on Farmer Friendly's farm. If Rico Shay's feet had not skidded to a stop, he would have bumped right into Benny Beagle.

"What and who are you?" blurted Rico Shay.

"I'm a dog," replied Benny. "I'm a beagle dog," he continued. "A beagle dog is a rabbit dog. That means that I am supposed to eat you."

Gulp! Went Rico Shay as he swallowed hard and frightened out of his wits at the thought of being eaten.

"Well, you don't look dangerous to me. Couldn't we become friends and just run races or something?" asked Rico Shay.

"No way," replied Benny Beagle. "My mother told me that beagle dogs can never become a friend of a rabbit."

"Well, you'll never catch me," boasted Rico Shay Rabbit. "I'll leave you standing in your tracks." Having said that, he moved away so fast that it made Benny Beagle's eyes blur.

"You won't get away," shouted Benny Beagle. "I have a very sensitive nose. I can smell you no matter where you go."

"You'll have to catch me first," shouted Rico Shay. "You can't catch smells and you can't eat them. Most of all, you can't catch me either."

From that day onward, the races between Benny Beagle and Rico Shay Rabbit never ended. Rico Shay learned that Benny was very slow and that he was not very smart, but he knew that Benny was very dangerous for him. Benny was very determined and he never stopped trying to catch Rico Shay. What was most dangerous was Benny's sensitive nose which could track Rico Shay's every step. Besides that, Benny hunted Rico Shay both day and night, so Rico Shay had to become a light sleeper and to always stay alert. Why do dogs have to be that way, thought Rico Shay? He, himself, was a nice fellow who wouldn't harm anyone.

A very strange thing happened one day during late summer. Farmer Friendly and twenty four other men arrived at the cabbage field. Farmer Friendly and three of the other men were driving four noisy machines called tractors. Each tractor was pulling two large wagons with high sideboards all around. The noise made by the tractors was so loud that Rico Shay's nerves were jangled. He had never been so frightened.

The men driving the tractors parked one at each corner of the field pointed in the same direction. As they began moving slowly forward, five men with long sharp knives began following each tractor, lopping the roots off each cabbage head and tossing them into the wagons. That happened so quickly that Rico Shay realized that he was surrounded. What was worse, Benny Beagle came with the men.

At first, it was easy for Rico Shay to outsmart Benny by staying near the middle of the large field, but, with each pass of the tractors, Rico Shay's hiding place became smaller and smaller Benny was barking now becoming more shrill and his excitement grew as he closed in on poor Rico Shay.

The men yelled to each other, "There's a rabbit in there."

Benny could see Rico Shay all the time now and kept barking as he tried to keep up with Rico Say's zig zag running. Rico Shay was growing very tired as the cabbage patch became smaller, he was running nearly all the time without a chance to rest. Each time he tried to break out into the newly cleared field, the men with the knives chased him back. Finally the cabbage patch became so small, the men parked all four of the tractors and the men came toward the frightened rabbit from all sides. With knives! And there stood Benny Beagle with his mouth open and his large red tongue dangling out of his mouth! Oh! How dreadful! Even Farmer Friendly did not look friendly.

The men kept pressing forward. Rico Shay Rabbit had to think fast and also act fast. He bagan running in a circle so fast that it made Benny Beagle so dizzy that he simply fell to the ground. Rico Shay then began running a zig zag route criss crossing inside the circle of men. They dashed and grabbed at the rabbit, but all that they tackled was each other. They became a heap of squirming scrambling men looking very much like football players trying to recover a fumble.

107

Had anyone bothered to look across the field near the edge of a large briar patch, rolling upon the ground with wild laughter, they would have seen Rico Shay Rabbit having the most fun of his young life.

Rico Shay Rabbit was much wiser now. He made up his mind that he would never allow himself to become surrounded by danger again.

He also thought that Farmer Friendly's farm was where he wanted to spend the rest of his life. After all, there was plenty of rabbit food and what better sport could there be than outsmarting dim witted Benny Beagle?

GRANDPA ED'S BEDTIME STORIES

AWESOME POSSUM

BY JAMES E. MARTIN

James E. Martin

AWESOME POSSUM

Awesome Possum never amounted to much, but he didn't care. The way he looked at life, why make waves? He thought that what will be will be anyway without any effort by him. The fact was, Awesome Possum was just plain lazy.

It started when he was a baby. For the first six weeks of his life, he and his eight brothers and sisters were carried about by their mother inside a warm leather fur-lined pouch attached to the outside of their mother's tummy. That was easy for her to do, because each of her babies were only as big as a bumble bee at first. Inside the pouch was so snug and dark that the babies could not even see daylight. With nine growing babies inside that pouch, it soon became crowded, so one by one, the babies moved out of that pouch and saw their mother for the very first time. My! how those babies had grown. Now they were almost as large as a mouse!

Do you know that possums have almost fifty teeth? They are very white and they are very sharp. Have you ever heard someone say, "Grin like a possum?" Well, that is something a possum really likes to do. They grin a lot. If you had fifty teeth, your mouth would look like a piano key board when you smiled. That is what Awesome Possum's mother did when she saw how her handsome babies had grown. She just smiled and smiled.

True to Awesome's lazy nature, he was the last of the babies to leave the comfort of that warm pouch, so he was also able to drink more of his mother's milk than the others. He became bigger and bigger. Before long, there was not enough room in the pouch for him either, so he had to come out. His mother had become vexed with him because of his laziness, so one day she just reached inside that pouch and yanked him out! She plopped him down upon the ground and she wasn't grinning, either.

Mother possum was about to scold him for being so lazy. She glared at him down her long narrow snout with her beady little black eyes when she drew in a long breath with amazement.

"Awesome!" she said. "That's what he is. Awesome! That is the biggest baby possum I have ever seen."

So that is how he got his name. From that day onward, he was known as Awesome Possum.

Now, there is something else that you should know about possums. They have very strong hairless tails. They are so strong that a possum can hang from a limb with their tails just as a monkey can. When a mother possum goes searching for food, goes down to a stream bank to get water, or goes to visit neighbors, she cannot leave her babies behind. If she did, a hawk, an owl, or maybe fox would find them and eat them. They are much too large to carry inside the pouch any longer. Even if they could get inside the pouch, mother possum's legs would have no room to operate. So she tells her babies to climb upon her back. She arches her powerful tail above her back and the little babies hang by their tails from her tail. It looks very much like a possum clothes line. With that arrangement, Mother Possum can go where ever she wishes while the babies also go for a ride.

Well, that is the way it was supposed to work, but every time that Awesome tired to swing from his mother's tail, her poor tail could not carry the load. Every time he joined the others, her tail would collapse, sending all of the babies tumbling along the ground. The same thing happened time after time. Besides, Awesome was so long that he did not have room to hang from his mother's tail anyway. Friends, you know that situation really tried Mother Possum's patience. Time after time the babies tumbled to the ground. Finally, with a sigh of disgust, she told Awesome just to ride between her shoulders so that the others could swing from her tail.

As the babies grew, Mrs. Possum became more and more weary of carrying the awful load. Besides, it became more hard work for her to find food enough for her family. Awesome by himself could eat as much as an adult possum. One day when she was near collapse from her heavy burden, she had a great idea. Since Awesome was so much bigger than any of his brothers and sisters, and since he was already half as large as his mother, why not require him to carry two or three of the babies hanging from his tail? It was important that Mother Possum survived so that she could provide food for her family. Should she die from exhaustion, who would take care of her babies? With Awesome helping to take care of the family she reasoned, perhaps he would learn lessons about good citizenship and become considerate of others.

We have already learned that Awesome was lazy. His mother's new plan worked well for a while, but Awesome soon grew tired of the responsibility. He was lazy, but he wasn't dumb. The way he saw it, why make a long trip for water and food each day instead of moving close to where it was found. He realized that he was almost as large as an adult possum and was continuing to grow rapidly. He really did not care for anyone but himself. He would just leave his family and live alone.

Awesome's mother had shown her family where a farmer grew a large vegetable garden. It contained all of the food which possums liked. Since possums nearly always travel at night and sleep all day, they can eat the farmers vegetables without being seen. In addition to that, Awesome found the den of a fat old ground hog not far from the garden. He would just move into the ground hog's den. That way, he would't have to work to dig his own den. He merely convinced the ground hog that he was no match for Awesome's mouth full of sharp teeth. So the ground hog moved out.

Well, everything seemed to be going just fine for Awesome. He enjoyed sleeping all day inside the cool safety of his stolen den for which he hadn't worked. He was getting all of the stolen food he wanted without having to work for it. He was also getting all of the water he needed from a watering trough used by the farmer to water his farm animals. Life was really good. He was not bothered by the hot daytime sun as he slept in the den located beneath a large rock. He enjoyed the balmy nights in the garden. He even enjoyed the cool refreshing rain when it fell. In his selfish way, he did not even care what had become of his family.

Usually, possums can run swiftly if danger appears. With a mouth full of fifty sharp teeth, Awesome had little to fear. But, one dark night when Awesome was raiding the farmer's garden, he was caught by total surprise when a powerful beam of light suddenly came on revealing Awesome in the act of stealing vegetables. The farmer had grown angry about whatever or whoever had been stealing his vegetables. Whoever it was had been very greedy as well as very inconsiderate, because the thief always selected the very finest vegetables. What was even worse, he would take a bite out of one vegetable and then more to take a bite out of another, then another, thus spoiling the vegetables for everyone else. That showed that Awesome was not only a greedy thief, but that he had very bad manners.

Awesome was so surprised that he didn't know what to do. He was cut off from escape to his den and, besides that, the farmer was accompanied by a very nasty looking coon hound! Awesome had never seen a dog before, so he was really frightened. The farmer shouted to the dog, "Sick 'im, Fritz!"

The dog attacked immediately ignoring Awesome's fifty grinning teeth of defiance. He moved right in and grabbed Awesome by the back of his neck and began shaking him violently like an old rag.

The farmer said, "OK, Fritz. That's enough" upon which the dog threw Awesome to the ground.

Awesome was scared, but he wasn't badly hurt, because possums are very difficult to injure. They can tolerate much pain and continue to live. We learned earlier that Awesome was not dumb. The fact is that possums are very clever. That was when Awesome did something which he had never done before. He played possum. That means that he pretended to be dead. He just lay there on the ground with his eyes closed and didn't even show any signs of breathing.

The farmer said, "Good boy, Fritz." He picked Awesome up by his tail. Awesome was just as limp as a wet mop. The farmer carried him over to a deep trash barrel, raised the lid, and dropped him inside.

Things were looking very bad for Awesome Possum, but his story did not end there. He was trapped inside that dark old trash barrel surrounded by smelly rubbish. Awesome pretended to be dead for a while after hearing the farmer and Fritz walk away. He didn't want to take a chance of making any noise for fear that they would come back. He just remained motionless for a long time until he was certain that it would be safe to try to escape. At last he stretched himself full length standing on his back legs while trying to claw his way out of the barrel, but without success. The wall of the barrel was too high. That was the hardest work that lazy Awesome had ever done, so he soon exhausted himself. He finally accepted his fate and lay atop the rubbish and went to sleep. At least he was alive and was not badly injured from the mauling he took from Fritz. He would just wait for morning to see what happened.

Awesome was awakened during early morning by the sound of a truck motor which was running nearby. He heard a man yell, "Hold it right there, Joe." Suddenly, Awesome felt the sensation of the barrel being lifted high into the air. The lid swung open as the barrel was turned upside down and the contents of the barrel were dumped over the high side boards of the truck bed. Awesome made a soft landing atop more rubbish as he became covered by that which was inside the barrel. Once more he was greatly frightened, but just as before, he played possum and did not as much as move a whisker.

Fortunately for Awesome, neither of the men saw him in the darkness. He felt safe for now. He nearly went out of his mind with fright when the truck motor began to roar and it sped down the highway. Time after time, Awesome had to dig his way from beneath rubbish as the men gathered trash from house after house along their route. Time after time, Awesome was clunked on his head by falling cans, bottles, chunks of wood, and an endless collection of other junk. He rode in that truck all day, remaining out of sight, when during the late afternoon, the truck arrived at a land fill.

Awesome could hear the voices of other men as they greeted the two who were in the truck. He could also hear the awful roar of heavy earth moving equipment operating nearby. He heard a man yell instructions to the truck driver, "Dump your load over yonder in that open pit that is not nearly full. I'll bury that one when it fills up tomorrow."

The truck was moved into position, when the bed suddenly tilted steeply and Awesome felt the entire load of rubbish go sliding into the deep pit. For a brief time, he felt as though he was tumbling over Niagara Falls until he struck the bottom of the pit once more suffering the indignity of being covered by smelly garbage. But, how lucky could Awesome be? He was not injured. All that he had to do was stay out of sight, avoid being buried by loads being dumped by other trucks, and await nightfall when he could climb over the great heaps of rubbish and excape.

Awesome was soon to discover that he had happened upon another great piece of luck. By looking about among the scraps of food contained in the rubbish, he discovered that there was an endless supply of the things that possums loved to eat. What was more, more of that food supply would be arriving every day of the year! He had to ask himself, have I really landed in Possum Paradise? Once more, lazy Awesome did not have to work for a living. All that remained for him to do was to locate a nice den in which to live.

It did not take long for Awesome to learn that there was a very large community of other animals already living at the land fill. There were many more possums, racoons, rats, foxes, mice, minks, weasels, and an occasional wandering bear. Many of the animals were lookling for the same things to eat which Awesome liked, but there was very little strife, because the new daily arrival of supplies was endless.

At first, Awesome had a bit of trouble finding a suitable place to live, but that did not take long. Awesome discovered a long hollow log lying along a hillside above a ravine near the landfill. There was only one slight problem; some other possums were already living inside the log. I say the problem was slight, because Awesome was awesome. He was huge! When the other possums saw Awesome's fifty sharp white teeth grinning at them in the darkness inside that log, they moved out of his reach without a fight, allowing him to have the choice section of the log as his home. To his way of thinking, his new home was a luxury hotel. With that problem settled, Awesome Possum soon adapted to his new surroundings and lived a long happy life.

BUTTERCUPS

It was the time of year when Great Meadow lay frozen and covered by a blanket of snow. The field was cold and shivering with its only visitors the North Wind, an occasional coton-tail rabbit, and the Sun who peeped over the tree tops once every several days. On some days, a red-tailed hawk making his schreeching sound would circle high into the sky. Strange as it may seem, Great Meadow was less lonely at night, when the mournful howls of wolves or the yapping of a fox echoed through the deep forest and towering mountains.

Gone were the sweet odor of clover blossoms and pretty yellow buttercups which grew in vast carpets upon the meadow during spring and summer. Gone, too, were the song birds and the butterflies. Not to be seen were the white puffy clouds floating through the bright blue sky, the warm sunshine, and the Babbling Brook. Great Meadow also missed the frolicking lambs, the young calves, and the gentle old cows who grazed upon the sweet flowers. Most of all, Great Meadow was lonesome for the three pretty little farmer's daughters who romped among the field dasies and buttercups.

Great Meadow wondered if they missed her too. She wondered if they would ever return to picnic upon the grass and then gather their basket full of clover, daisies, and buttercups to take home to their Mommie and their Granny. Was their visits to Great Meadow a passing childhood fancy? Would they forget the fun they had? Would they be too grown-up to gather wild flowers, to float petals in Babbling Brook like little boats? Would they no longer squeal with delight when startled by a green frog or imagine that they were watching a real live fairy when they saw a dragon fly go flitting past? Would t hey ever come back to race with the wooly lambs, the frisky calves, or to feed sugar cubes to the bay colt? Oh! Why did winter have to last so long?

The lonely days dragged by with howling winds and drifting snow. The wind blew so hard across the sky that on some nights, the moon and the clouds seemed to be having a race. There also were some nights when the moon did not shine, but in its place were millions of stars whose bright points of light looked like the tip ends of icicles.

A day came at last when Mr. Sun popped his warm smiling face over the rims of the mountains. He beamed down upon Great Meadow, his warm rays causing the snow to thaw and the ice on Babbling Brook to melt. When Great Meadow began to awaken from her long winter nap, she could feel the tingle of little rivlets of water seeping into her soil. It caused a delightful tickling feeling as she realized that she was coming to life once more. As she opened her sleepy eyes and saw the blanket of snow being lifted from her bed, could what she saw really be true? Were those little bright red dots popping up everywhere the heads of earthworms peeping out to see if Spring had really arrived. And was that a robin red breast hopping upon her chest? As she looked about, Great Meadow was thrilled to hear the clear musical tinkle of melting water rushing once more over the rocks in Babbling Brook. She also heard the first chirps of the green frogs. She knew that it would not be long before the first yellow buttercups would be in bloom. It also would not be long before Farmer Friendly would open the meadow gate. Lambs would be racing ahead of their mothers to play games of topsy turvey among themselves. The young calves would also arrive running stiff-legged, with their ears perked forward, and their tails pointed skyward straight up over their backs. The Mama Cows would come waddling along wagging their bodies as they munched mouths-full of sweet clover.

Great Meadow's joy knew no bounds as that scene unfolded, but there were some nagging questions which caused uneasiness to linger. Would those darling little girls return this year? If so when? The winter had been so long, so time now without them seemed to stand still. Great doubts disturbed Great Meadow. Maybe they had moved away and would never come back. That would be so sad.

Then one warm day in June after school had been closed for the summer, Great Meadow's heart almost burst with joy. At first, the distant sound of little giggles carried upon a breeze was just barely audible. Then came another, closer and more distinct this time. Almost at once, just as plain as day, came a burst of pure laughter as only a little girl can produce. The little girls had not forgotten – they were returning to visit their old friend. Soon they came into sight, running and holding hands. They plopped down upon a great mound of yellow buttercups. One opened the picnic basket and spread a small table cloth upon the ground. It was not before a circle of curious little calves and wolly lambs ringed the little girls, making sure that they did not miss any of the excitement.

When the picnic was over, the little girls spent the afternoon playing chase with the calves and lambs. Before returning home, they removed their shoes and held up their skirts as they waded the cool water of

Babbling Brook. Once more, they giggled and squealed when green frogs sprang off the banks of the brook and splashed into the water near their feet. When Mr. Sun began to hide his face once more behind the mountain tops, the little girls took time to fill their picnic basket with fragrant flowers to take home to their Mommie and their Granny. They took a moment to glance back across the face of their good friend, Great Meadow, then skipped and laughed their way home.

As the peaceful twilight settled over the land, Great Meadow realized that hers was the best place on earth. A great horned owl hooted his agreement as Mr. Moon began to show his smiling face above the horizon. The wooly lambs and the calves were quiet now, cuddling with their Mommies and laying their little heads to sleep upon Great Meadow's breast.

Pleasant dreams,
GRANDPA ED.

GRANDPA ED'S BEDTIME STORIES

HELMUT

UND

GRETCHEN

BY JAMES E. MARTIN

HELMUT UND GRETCHEN

Helmut and Gretchen are just ordinary wooden nut-crackers, the kind that travelers often see in wood carvers' shops in the Black Forest of Germany. I selected them to buy from a shelf containing many others. I especially liked Helmut and Gretchen.

Helmut is fashioned to resemble a Captain of Emperor Wilhelm's palace guards. He wears a forest green uniform with large brass buttons, a wide black belt, tan trousers, a spiked helmet emblazoned on its front by Germany's National Symbol, a spread eagle. As was the style during Emperor Wilhelm's day, Helmut wears a big paint-brush style mustache. He also has a very large tummy.

Gretchen looks like a typical old peasant woman whose shoulders are stooped from too much hard work. She wears a drab brown ankle-length dress with a wrap-around apron, and a faded red poka-dot shawl draped over her head.

I shall tell you from the start that I never did think there was anything magical about that pair of nut-crackers. The were designed to crack nuts by placing a nut inside their mouths and crushing it by pushing down hard on a wooden level located behind their backs. There are many kinds of nut-crackers throughout the world; these two just happened to be designed to look like people. I was enchanted by them just as I was enchanted by the wood carver's entire shop on the day that I bought them. I brought them home with me to America where they have rested upon a book shelf in my study for many years.

If you ever travel to Germany's Black Forest, you shall discover that the forest, itself, is enchanting. So much so, that it gives one the feeling that there is something magical everywhere you look. In fact, many of the world's best fairy tales were written about that area, the story about Hansel and Gretel. There must also be some belief in the magical powers of nut-crackers to come to life in that part of the world, because one great composer of classical music wrote a composition titled 'The Nut-cracker Sweet'. Thousands of people crowd great concert halls each year to hear that fairy tale put to music.

Perhaps I should not be too mystified by the story that I am going to tell you, for we who are very old and you tiny tots who are very young know all about 'wee people' such as elves, and gnomes, trolls, and fairies

121

who live in cool dark forests and in fields filled with summertime daisies. So it happened very late one summer night when I was sitting in a big easy chair in my study. I was alone except for my old tabby cat who was alseep on the floor by my feet. My family had gone away from home on a visit. I had eaten a late supper before starting to read a book about days long ago when there were knights and castles and magic things. I shut everything else from my mind as I read about events of those ancient times. I read about kings and earls, maidens in distress, helpless children whose puppy dogs tried to defend them against fire breathing dragons, and about poor woodcutters who barely earned enough money to buy food to eat. I read about huge dark forests with only foot paths for roads, about little gingerbread cottages hidden among the trees, of wolves, bears, bambi deer, and fairy god-mothers. Through the window of my study, I could look outside at my own dark forest. My mind was filled with gentle thoughts about some enchanted land far away when some time late that night I fell to sleep in my comfortable easy chair.

I was awakened suddenly from my deep sleep by a powerful thunder storm. The storm came with torents of rain, swirling wind, and great flashes of lightning. The electricity had been knocked out. Except for the eerie flickers of lightning, the inside of my study was totally dark. Branches of the forest trees were violently threshing about in the wind while as assortment of wind chimes which my wife kept hanging from the low eaves of our house were playing a strange symphony of music as they tinkled in the wind.

With my thoughts having been filled by the enchantment of the wonderful stories that I had been reading, I was not certain if I was actually awake or if I were only dreaming. My first impulse was to dash to the window and look at the storm, but what I saw and heard caused me to fall back into my chair in wonderment. I absolutely could not believe my eyes. What was happening inside my study, be I awake or be it a dream, amazed me and caused my eyes to bulge.

While the storm raged outside, the wind-chimes made the strange sounding music, a loose shutter outside the window was beating what sounded like a steady drum-beat boom-de-boom, boom-de-boom. Inside the dark room, lit only by the storm's flashes of lightning through the windows, my eyes caught a glimpse of Helmut and Gretchen swirling about upon a bookshelf doing an old-fashioned German clog dance. That was where I had thought they had stood motionless for years! But, that was not all! As the lightning flickers danced about the darkened room, the mirrored walls of my wife's curio cabinet, whose shelves were loaded with Dresden figurines, ballerinas, and Hummel goose girls and boys, was alive with every one of them dancing to the beat of the music boom-de-boom-boom!

Upon another shelf inside the room, a porcelean goose, a pair of ceramic ducks with their flock of little babies, were all waddling back and forth. A stuffed cloth chicken as well as a stuffed cloth turkey which my wife had made were also nodding their heads in time with the music Boom-de-boom-boom! A fat old Monk in an oil painting hanging upon my study wall was smiling and patting his big tummy. A pair of Raggedy Ann and Andy dolls hanging from hooks on another wall were swaying with the music. A toy wagon parked next to the hearth was loaded with a family of Teddy Bears who were smiling.

A pair of Bambi Deer frightened by the storm had wandered out of the forest to shelter themselves by the outside wall of the house were watching the show through a window. I felt a stir at my feet where my old Tabby Cat had been sleeping. She was stretching her legs and did a rumba dance across the carpet Boom-de-boom-boom. I just sat there throughout that marvelous show in amused bewilderment, for I could see that I had nothing to dread.

Just as I was hoping that wonderful scene would never end, the electricity suddenly came back on and filled the room with light. The lights frightened the deer who quickly returned to the forest. The storm passed as suddenly as it had began and all of the fairyland creatures became silent and motionless where they had always been.

Old Tabby Cat pussyfooted back across the room slowly swishing her tail. She looked up at me and meowed in what sounded like "Milk" as she moved in the direction of the kitchen while looking back to see if I was following.

After I gave Tabby some milk, I went to bed where I had wonderful dreams about deep dark forests and paths lined by tall ferns. I dreamed of whispy water falls, of cottages made of gingerbread, of Wee People, of fairies, woodland animals, and of magical nut-crackers. Through it all, the dying winds of the storm only seemed to make me sleep sounder.

Now, Kiddies, I have never told any 'grown-ups' about what happened that wonderful night, because most 'grown-ups' might think that such a thing cannot happen. But, little children such as you are and Old Grandpas such as I am know all about magic forests and the woodland creatures who come out to play when the time is just right. The time is just right when little children are going to bed and Mommies, Daddies, and Grandparents are reading bedtime stories. Who knows? Maybe some time the fairyland people will invite you to join them just like Alice In Wonderland or Dorothy in The Wizard of Oz.

Happy dreams to you,
Grandpa Ed

BLACK COTTON

BY JAMES E. MARTIN

James E. Martin

BLACK COTTON

Once there was a Mother Rabbit who had three little baby bunnies. Just as their mother, two of the bunnies were snow white with pink noses, pink eyes, and pink ears, but the third bunny did not have a single white hair. He was as black as coal all over. The only things that made him look like the other bunnies was that he was shaped like a rabbit, he had a power-puff tail, and he had long rabbit ears.

When the bunnies were born, Mother Rabbit thought they looked like little balls of cotton. It would be easy for her to give names such as Snow, Cottontail, or Pearl to the white ones, but what could she name the little black bunny? He certainly was fuzzy like a little ball of cotton, but who had ever seen black cotton? She smiled to herself when she thought how strange a field of black cotton would look. Then she thought what a good name that would be for the little black bunny.

She said out loud, "I'll name him Black Cotton."

Black Cotton was a great favorite among the other bunnies who also lived near his home. He grew to be a very large handsome rabbit and was great fun to have as a playmate. He ran very fast when the bunnies played a game of tag. He was also very hard to catch, because he could change direction so quickly it caused the other bunnie's eyes to pop. When the bunnies played hide-and-seek, the white ones had trouble hiding themselves where they could not be seen, but it was easy for Black Cotton to hide himself. All that he had to do was press his body tightly against the ground, flatten his ears against his back, close his bright eyes so the others could not see them shine. When he did that, Black Cotton was very hard to find.

Sometimes, Black Cotton would tease his Mother by hiding from her, but Mother Rabbit was a wise old bunny who knew all of the tricks. All that she had to do to bring him out of hiding was to carry a bundle of blooming clover, a paw full of plump fresh carrots, or a head of tasty cabbage near his hiding place. Once Black Cotton's sensitive nose smelled the scent of his favorite foods, his tummy always urged him not to miss the chance to eat a snack. The trick always worked. He would come out of hiding and would bunny hop along beside Mother Rabbit begging for a tasty treat.

126

Mother Rabbit worried about the safety of her little family. She had to teach the young bunnies about the danger of crossing roads and to stay away from foxes, dogs, cats, snakes, and hawks who are not friendly with rabbits. She also warned them to stay out of boxes and cages which may actually be traps. Although most of rabbit's favorite foods are grown by gardeners, people do not approve of rabbits helping themselves to their vegetables. For that reason, most rabbits do something very naughty. They sneak into vegetable gardens at night and steal food for which they did not work. As you know, stealing is a big no-no, for stealing is wrong. But that is a 'man thing' which rabbits do not understand. They just know that they like vegetables and will eat them where ever they find them.

Mother Rabbit also warned her babies that dogs, cats, and foxes have great sense of smell and that they use their noses to find rabbits no matter how hard they are to see. Besides, cats can see in the dark!

As time passed, the baby rabbits wandered farther and farther from home. They visited old houses, gopher holes, hollow logs, and best of all, vegetable gardens where carrots, lettuce, and cabbage grew.

As the bunnies grew, they left home and went their separate ways. Black Cotton traveled far and wide, visiting many strange places. Once, having climbed a high bluff at night, Black Cotton found himself looking down at the bright lights of a large city. A broad river flowed through the city and one of its bends passed by a large city park which bordered the steep hill upon which Black Cotton stood. Black Cotton could hear happy music coming from somewhere in the park, and his sensitive nose could smell the wonderful odor of hot popcorn, roasting peanuts, and the wonderful odor of cotton candy. He could hear the excited voices and the laughter of many children who seemed to be having great fun. The sounds and smells seemed to be coming from the area near the foot of the hill, but clumps of bushes and stones which jutted out from the edge of the steep bluff blocked his view. He wanted to see what all of the excitement was about, so he crept nearer and ever nearer the edge hoping to get a clear view.

At last he reached a small ledge from which he was looking down at the top of a huge circus tent and several smaller ones scattered around it. To him, the scene was a magic wonderland – the bright lights, the noise, the odors, the music, hundreds of people milling about. He saw children, and monkeys, lions, tigers, elephants, and giraffes. He saw many colors of balloons, banners, colorfully dressed silly clowns, men on stilts, poodle dogs wearing hats and dresses, kangaroos wearing top hats, bears riding tricycles, and fancy ladies riding upon the backs of horses wearing tall feather plumes on top of their heads. Just at the moment when Black Cotton stretched a bit further to see if there were any rabbits, he lost his balance!

Poor Black Cotton! At first he felt himself falling! Falling! Falling! Suddenly his body struck the sloping side of a small tent. He went sliding down the side of that tent with his body rolled up like a ball. He shot off the tent and went rolling across a narrow lane right under the edge of the Circus Big Top tent. Looking like a black ball, he rolled and rolled across the floor of that huge tent until he came to rest against the leg of the Circus Ring Master!

The Ring Master was just starting to announce the opening act of a group of toy poodles who were going to perform a tumbling act. The poodles were not much bigger than Black Cotton. When the crowd saw the wildly funny and unexpected entrty of poor Black Cotton, they thought that he was part of the poodle act. They thought that it was so funny, they stood upon their feet and cheered and cheered!

The Ring Master didn't have to act surprised, he really was. He picked the dazed Black Cotton up and held him out at arms length and asked, "What do we have here?"

The Ring Master could tell that Black Cotton had had a very scary experience, so he handed the poor rabbit to a very tall happy looking clown and said, "Take this furry fellow to see the Circus Doctor to treat him for any injuries and then put him into a small cage where he will be safe from harm."

The kind doctor gave Black Cotton a warm bath, then treated his scratches and bruises after which a circus girl made him a comfortable bed inside a small cage. After the show ended that night, the Ring Master and the Doctor came to visit Black Cotton.

The Ring Master asked, "What are we going to do with him? He would be in great danger if we turn him lose in the city."

"Why not keep him with the Circus for the rest of the summer season?" asked the Animal Doctor. "He would become a great Favorite as a part of the children's petting zoo, and besides, the Animal Trainer might work him into one of the small animal acts."

"I think that is a good idea," said the Ring Master. "And, when the season is over, I can turn him loose with the other bunnies inside my big back yard at home where my children will take care of him."

So Children, that is how a tiny bunny grew to become the famous Black Cotton The Magnificant in the Greatest Show On Earth.

Yours truly with Country Love
Grandpa Ed.

WARTY, THE WARTHOG

BY JAMES E. MARTIN

WARTY, THE WARTHOG

Even on the day that he was born, it was hard to imagine that any animal could be as ugly as Warty Warthog. Ofcourse, with him being an animal, he never realized that he was ugly. He did not just one day pop his eyes open and say, "Hey! Everybody look how ugly I am!" But, Warty, just as is true with humans, he had no choice whatever if he was going to be a warthog or something else. He just happened to be born into a family of one of the ugliest creatures on earth. Maybe if he had a choice, he would have been one of the earth's lovely creatures such as a puppy or a kitten.

But wait. Who am I to say that Warty was ugly? My opinion of how he looks is through the eyes of a human and my opinion does not make any difference at all. Where Warty lives in Central Africa, the other animals do not care how he looks. To the other warthogs, he may be very handsome. It is certain that to the other animals, how he looks is not important. Only fault-finding humans such as myself would complain about his appearance.

Now, it is certain that you are never going to see a warthog in high society, riding a subway or a school bus, or shopping at a mall. You will not see one at church, at a ball game, or at a dance. That is right; Warty and his family are going to remain out of the sight of the human world contended to spend their lives in Central Africa.

As warthogs go, Warty was a good little pig. He learned to eat plants, nuts, fruit, bugs, bird eggs, and roots. He enjoyed wallowing in loose sand and in gooy mud holes. That was as close as he ever came to taking a bath.

When Warty became full grown, he would weigh almost two hundred pounds, his body would be covered by wrinkled grey skin, and he would wear a mane of long red hair along the back of his neck and the entire length of his spine. His legs would be short with sharp pointed toes. His small ears would stand straight up and his eyes would buldge out in such a manner that he could see behind himself without turning his head. A warthog gets its name because of three large warts which grow atop its long snout. Long sharp ugly tusks grow out of their lower jaws, the ends of which rise several inches above their snouts.

131

Warty also had a twin sister named Wartina. Both of them being wartpigs, they looked very much alike. At the time they were born, their parents were making a long journey to the lower fringe of a great African desert where they could escape the rising flood waters of the African rainy season. The little pigs ran squealing helter-skelter as they frolicked among the bushes and tall grass as they moved along with thousands of many kinds of other animals who were also escaping from the great floods. There was much danger of being stepped upon or even eaten by much larger animals. The journey to the high grounds took many days and the distance traveled was many miles. The rain kept falling and the water was gathering in the low places. Rivers were becoming swift and deep. The earth was churned into disgusting mud by the millions of tramping hooves and feet. Gone now were the bushes and the tall grass. All had either been eaten or trampled into the mud. As the food supply disappeared, most of the animals were very hungry.

Now that there were more and more streams everywhere every day, a new and terrible danger appeared each time the warthog family reached a river bank. Mean old crocodiles and very large snakes who lived there all of the time just waited for small animals such as Warty and his sister to come near enough to be eaten.

As the days passed and the many miles were behind the travelers, the land began to rise toward the desert, fewer and more narrow streams appeared, and the heavy rain began to slacken. The crowded herds of animals began to spread out, and the animals began to find enough food to avoid starving. The warthogs, hoping to avoid being crushed by the larger animals, pushed on nearer to the edges of the desert where they could find huge termite hives, ground nesting birds, and shrubs with shallow roots to eat. This new home would be only temporary at most, because, when the floods went away, the warthogs would return to their home regions where food was in greater supply.

They had lived in their new home only a few days when a strange sight appeared upon the horizon. At first, it appeared as a cloud of dust, but as the hours passed, they could see a large caravan of camels come into plain view. As the tall camels swayed to and fro slowly plodding along in the desert sand bearing their huge loads of merchandise, the bells they wore around their necks, the pots, pans, and other items tinkled and clanged with each step. Fierce looking Arabs, some riding, many walking; some wearing broad curved swords swung from their belts, glared with lazer-like sternness in all direction as if they were guarding against an attack by bandits or wild animals. Most of the men had black beards, wore brightly colored scarves on their heads, were dressed in long loose-fitting robes, and wore strap sandals on their feet. There were hundreds of men, but only a few women and small children. All of the women were dressed in black with matching scarves covering their heads and all of their faces except their eyes. The children were barefooted and wore knee length smocks with a cord tied around their waists.

Along with many camels, there were some goats and some very vicious dogs. The dogs were what greatly frightened the warthogs. Although the warthogs hid themselves among the bushes and large rocks, the dogs keen sense of smell told them just where the warthogs were hiding. Warty's parents soon learned that they could not defend themselves from so many dogs, so they swiftly fled to escape. The caravan halted as the Arabs on foot chased poor Warty and Wartina until they caught them. The piglets had never seen either men, camels, or dogs before. They were struggling and squealing with terror when caught.

The wicked men swooped each of them up and held them at arms length as they grinned at them with snaggled teeth. The frightened piglets soon found themselved fastened inside a wooden crate and were hoisted atop the back of a tall camel. The sheik who owned the caravan grinned and said, "I know where those pigs will fetch a good price." He then signaled for the caravan to move onward.

Days passed slowly as the caravan crossed the hot desert before arriving at an old village called Timbuktu. It was what is called an oasis where the people and animals of the caravan drank the first water they had seen in days. Warty and Wartina were given dates and pieces of palm frons to eat along with water to drink.

After two days of rest, the caravan moved across the desert once more. A week later they reached a port town on the shore of the Nile River. The port was a busy place where many more people, camels, horses, donkeys, goats, dogs, cats, and chickens milled about. The poor piglets were too frightened to make a sound amid all of the confusion. They just cowered in the crate and tried not to attract attention. That was not easy when nasty dogs came sniffing at them between the slats of the crate.

The great burdens carried by the camels were unloaded at a huge out-door market where thousands of merchants and traders bought and sold goods of many kinds. There were blankets, scarves, necklaces, baskets, goat-skin water bottles, sunglasses, perfume, olive oil, rope, and camel saddles. There were pots, pans, sandals, and many kinds of terrible looking knives. Some of the men from the caravan sold elephant tusks, rhinoceros horns, spears, shields made of tree bark, jewelry made of animal teeth, and even live monkeys and snakes. One man had a vicious live cheetah for sale. It was a small wonder then when men who were wanting to buy wild animals bargined for the purchase of the warthog piglets. They were sold along with the other animals, birds, and snakes.

That night, Warty and Wartina were loaded aboard a large river boat along with the other animals and a large cargo of African goods. They were soon sailing down the great Nile River enroute to the large city of Cairo, Egypt. By that time, the frightened little piglets thought that their world had been turned upside down. Oh! If only they were still running free with their parents in the great wilderness!

After a week, the animals were off-loaded upon a pier at Cairo where once more they were taken to a large market place. For the first time, a very nice man came to see Warty and his sister. He kneeled beside their crate and said, "Hi guys. How would you like to become my Friends?"

The nice man told the Arab merchant that he would buy the piglets. As soon as he paid for them, he had his helper move each of them into separate small plastic carrying cases with floors covered by straw mattresses. Soon the piglets were loaded into the back of a station wagon. Once more they were scared out of their wits by the roar of the engine. It was not long before they were taken out of the station wagon and were loaded upon a huge jet plane! Needless to say, when that plane took off, those poor pigs were sure that the world had come to its end. It was not long before they became calm once more. It was a long ride, so they went to sleep. After many hours, they were awakened by the sound of many voices and the sound of engines outside the plane. The cargo doors were opened and there stood their new friend. Their cases were handed to him and he placed them once more into the back of a station wagon. This time, the piglets were no longer frightened. They were 'getting the hang' of this sort of travel. It seemed to be only a short ride from the airport to what was to become their new home, The National Zoo at Washington, D.C. where to this very day Warty and Wartina are living happily ever after.

WOODROW NEVER WAS HERE

James E. Martin

WOODROW NEVER WAS HERE

Woodrow was a real mystery in the little village of Valley Bend. If he did everything that people accused him of, he was a very bad boy. He began getting the blame for everything that went wrong one day when Granny Olson placed a plum pie upon an outside window sill to cool so that it would be ready for her family's supper. When Granny went to get it, the pie was gone!

Little Cory, her four year old grandson, had an imaginary playmate whom he called Woodrow. Cory was often overheard talking to Woodrow as he played by himself in the yard, but the adults did not pay much attention to that. So, when Granny announced that her pie was stolen from her kitchen window sill, little Cory said, "Granny, I know who took your pie. It must have been Woodrow."

"If that is true, that Woodrow must be a very naughty boy," said Granny. Somebody should tell his parents about him. I don't think that you should play with him any more, Cory."

After a short pause, Granny continued, "There is something else, Woodrow must be very greedy. He ate that whole pie right where it was and left the plate on the window sill!"

Everyone in Cory's family was sad, because they really liked Granny's plum pies.

It was not long before poor Woodrow was blamed again. This time, Cory's Mommie had packed a tasty picnic lunch for Cory and his Daddy to take with them to the river when they went fishing. Cory's Daddy set the picnic basket on top of a flat rock near a clump of bushes, while they went to the river bank to fish. When they returned to the basket to eat lunch, the lunch was not there! Except for a few scraps, the basket was empty! The fishermen were amazed.

"Who could have eaten so much lunch by himself?" asked Cory's Daddy.

"I think I know. Woodrow has been here," said Cory. "That Woodrow is acting like a bad boy. If that's the way he is going to act, I just may not play with him any more!"

"How big is that Woodrow fellow, anyway?" asked Cory's Daddy.

"He's not much bigger than I am, but I do not know how old he is," replied Cory.

"Where does he live? I'd like to talk to his parents," said Cory's Daddy.

"I don't know," replied Cory, "But he spends a lot of time up in trees."

The story about Woodrow soon spread throughout the village. It seemed that almost every family had a bad experience with him. Some said that he tore their trash bags open and scattered the contents upon the ground. Several gardeners complained that he sneaked into their gradens at night and stole their very finest ripe tomatoes and sweet corn. As though that was not bad enough, he broke the corn stalks down making it look as though the garden had been destroyed by a wind storm.

Mrs Brown called the Sheriff to report that Woodrow had shooed her old red hen off her nest and had stolen a dozen eggs which she was hoping to hatch. Mr. Robinson reported that Woodrow had stolen most of his large ripe strawberries right off the vine the very night before he was planning to take them to market.

Mrs. Cary Kooter said that naughty boy had crept into her cabbage patch. She was planning to use that cabbage to make sour kraut, but Woodrow had spoiled every head by eating large chunks out of the side of every head!

Woodrow must have had an appetite for almost every kind of food, because Mrs Conrad Carbunkle reported that he even ate all of the cat food that she placed upon her doorstep each night for her cat named Wampus.

The whole community was abuzz about the mysterious new stranger called Woodrow. The little village of Valley Bend was much too small to have a mayor and a police force. The nearest law enforcement officer was the Sheriff ten miles away at the County Seat at Carson Corner. As the mystery of Woodrow spread, people all across Carson County began calling the Sheriff complaining that the boy called Woodrow had raided their property. They demanded that the Sheriff begin a man-hunt to capture him. The Sheriff asked people to describe Woodrow, but they all said that he was far too cunning to allow himself to be seen.

The poor Sheriff was bewildered by all of the reports about the things Woodrow was supposed to have done. Actually, there was plenty of evidence to see, but every time that the Sheriff asked if anyone had actually seen Woodrow in the act, nobody had ever seen him. That Woodrow was one smart thief. Besides, he never struck at the same place twice. How could he strike in every part of the County without being seen? Since people all over were reporting damage and loss, what did

Woodrow use for transportation? If he traveled by car, how come he was never caught in a road-block? How could he just be everywhere? Could he fly?

The Sheriff announced a meeting to be held at the Carson County High School Auditorium one Friday night to discuss the problem and to ask citizens for their advice as to how to catch the thief. There was much angry shouting and demands for the Sheriff to do his job, but no solutions to the problem were offered. No one at the meeting had ever seen Woodrow. There was no way to tell when or where he would strike next. The biggest question of all was, how is the Sheriff going to catch someone whom he cannot see? The meeting broke up with everyone going home grumbling about a Sheriff who could not catch even one small thief.

The local newspaper, The Carson Corner Trumpet, had a large front page article about the elusive Woodrow. There was also a picture of Sheriff Selby whom they said was such a poor investigator that he couldn't catch a cold, much less a smart crook like Woodrow. Sheriff Selby paid no attention to the nasty remarks printed in the newspaper, but kept trying to solve the mystery as best he could under the circumstances.

Hoping that he might locate Woodrow's family, Sheriff Selby researched all of Carson County's birth records at the court house. He made an amazing discovery; not a single boy named Woodrow had been born there during the past fifteen years!

Angry citizens kept demanding that the Sheriff do whatever was necessary to find that thief and put him out of action. Who was the only person in Carson County who claimed that he had actually seen Woodrow? That person was little Cory

The Sheriff came to Cory's house and asked his parents' permission to talk to Cory. Cory had never seen a sheriff before, so he was excited to see his brightly painted car with the silver-colored siren and the many lights. He was also impressed by the Sheriff's brown uniform topped by a big 'Smokey Bear' hat.

Sheriff Selby asked, "Cory, do you know a boy named Woodrow?"

"Oh yes," replied Cory. "He is my friend."

"Really!" remarked the Sheriff, unable to hide his surprise. "When was the last time you saw him?"

"Just a little while before you came in," replied Cory. "I have been playing with him in our back yard all day."

The Sheriff stared at Cory with amazement! "Well, where is Woodrow now?" he asked.

Cory answered with excitement, "He should be waiting for me out in the yard. Would you like to see him? He is waiting for me to come back out to play."

All of the adults followed Cory outside. Cory called out to his friend, "Hey Woodrow, I am ready to play some more."

"Well, where is he?" demanded the Sheriff, becoming a bit irritated.

"Do you mean that you can't see him? Did you not hear him answer me when I called him?" asked Cory. "He is right in front of you sitting upon that limb of the weeping willow tree looking down at you."

"Well, I can't see anybody. Can you folks see anybody?" fumed the Sheriff.

All of Cory's kin folks admitted that they did not see anyone either. "How is he dressed?" asked the Sheriff.

Cory replied, "He is wearing a forest green shirt, brown overalls, little shoes with turned up toes, and a brown hat shaped like a haystack with a long grey feather stuck in the hatband. He has a long pointed beard, sparkling blue eyes under great bushy eyebrows. For you see, Woodrow is a leprechaun. Can adults not see leprechauns?" Cory pleaded.

All of the adults laughed and felt just a little bit guilty. How strange that they could forget that they once were little children who believed in leprechauns, elves, and fairies who, to them, were very real?

The wise old Sheriff patted Little Cory on his head and said, "I think I may have a clue as to whom our thief may be. Granny, if I came back to your house for supper, could you bake a couple of those good plum pies?"

"Why, of course," replied Granny. I shall be happy to."

When the Sheriff had returned and everyone had finished eating supper, darkness had fallen over the village when the Sheriff said, "Granny, I'm ready for you to give me that other plum pie now."

Granny gave him the pie. Cory and his Daddy followed the Sheriff out to his car, where he removed a large wire cage trap from the trunk. He carried the trap out to the back yard where he placed it upon the ground, inserted the pie for bait, and armed the trap door.

He said, "When I return in the morning, I think we will have caught the mystery thief. Thanks for supper. I'll see you in the morning."

Sure enough, just as he expected, right there inside the cage was one very large, extremely fat, shiny, healthy, well-fed raccoon! Granny's plum pie was only a plesant memory.

The Sheriff said, "Mystery solved. I'll carry him way down South of Meyer's Lake where he can live in peace. Unless Cory's Mom provides him another picnic basket, it is doubtful that he will ever feast upon plum pie again. Ha! Ha!."

So our story ends, for you see, WOODROW NEVER WAS HERE.

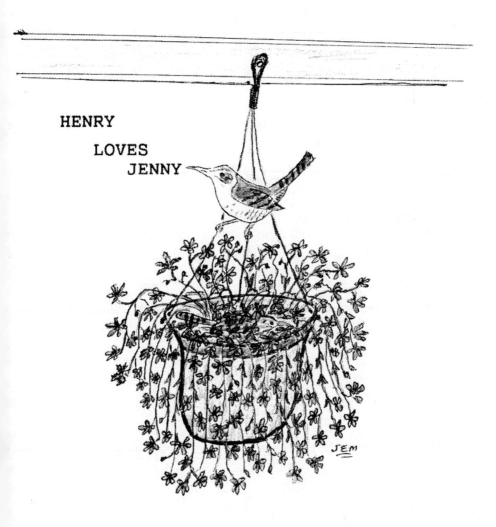

HENRY

LOVES

JENNY

James E. Martin

HENRY LOVES JENNY

Henry and Jenny were two tiny birds. They were brown house wrens. They were very young when they first met while traveling North into West Virginia during the early spring. Their families had spent the winter in the warm costal regions of the Gulf of Mexico. As their families settled in their new community, the two young lover's hearts were aflutter each time they met. Soon, they spent most of their time planning a home of their own.

Also during the early spring, Grandma Betty began hanging pots of pretty blooming flowers around the edge of her porch roof. She lives in a little house atop a small hill beside a forest. Some of the flowers contained red flowers, some were white, and other were a lovely pink. "What a wonderful nest one of those flower pots would make," Jenny told Henry. House wrens will build their nests inside almost any tiny sheltered place as long as the house is near a forest. They have been known to build their nests inside old abandoned shoes, a tin can, a hat, inside the open end of a pipe, a whole in a wall, and their favorite place is inside a pot of flowers. Who could blame them for that?

Grandma Betty was both amused and pleased when she saw Jenny and Henry perched upon the rim of one of her hanging pots. They were chattering excitely, poking their tiny heads beneath the leaves of the flowers, flitting their wings, and sticking their perky little tails almost straight up skyward. First one and then the other would disappear inside the flower pot. Their excitement reminded Grandma Betty of the time over fifty years ago when she and Grandpa Ed were sweethearts planning their lives together.

The flower pot hung in a sheltered place safe from falling rain, the pot was protected from the hot direct rays of the sun, and it hung where it could swing gently in the breeze. Oh! What a lovely place for a nest How happy the young lovers would be in their new home!

Now that they had agreed upon the location of their new home, the little birds began to fly in materials with which to build their nest from Granny's lawn and the surrounding forest. They spent all of the daylight hours of the following two days carrying soft thin straws of grass, each bird returning to the nest every few minutes until the nest was completed to their satisfaction.

Granny usually spends a few hours on summer afternoons sitting in her rocking chair on the back porch, either reading a magazine or hand sewing the beautiful quilts which she makes. She often smiled at the two tiny home makers who were fluttering in and out of her flower pot. She noticed that Jenny always lit upon the rim of the pot before entering the nest, but Henry always perched near the top of the wire from which the pot was hung. Each time, he would wrap his tiny toes around the wire and would slide down the wire much as a fireman slides down the metal pole inside the firehouse when the fire alarm is sounded. The great difference was that Henry slid down the wire headfirst and would disappear beneath the foliage of the flower.

After a few days of honeymoon, Jenny began laying one egg per day inside her nest. Granny knew that something special was happening, because Henry had started positioning himself upon a nearby limb for hours at a time as though he was on guard duty. If another bird came anywhere near, he would began to chatter loudly and would chase the intruder away. When Granny would see Jenny leave the nest, she would sneak a peek into the flower pot. The first day, Granny saw one tiny speckled egg about the size of a pinto bean. Three days later, the number of eggs had increased to four. Soon afterwards, when Granny looked into the nest, Jenny was always there. She was hovering over her eggs, silent as a stone, her feathers blending so perfectly with the color of the nest that she was almost invisible. Each time Granny wandered onto the porch, Henry became very much alarmed and made a terrible scolding racket.

Jenny sat upon her nest constantly day and night for almost two weeks. Henry was not idle during that time. He constantly carried food to Jenny, resting only long enough to talk to her with wren talk while perched upon a nearby tree branch.

Henry was a tiny little fellow, weighing only a few ounces, but he was very brave. His parents had taught him that some of the larger birds such as crows, grackles, starlings, and cat birds would eat the eggs and babies of little birds such as wrens. It was good that Jenny's nest was so well hidden inside Granny's flower pot. One of the greatest dangers to small birds were the red tailed hawks who sailed high above the ground. Their eyes have almost X-ray power, their beaks are razor sharp, as also are their sharp claws. They circle high above the ground making a shrill screeching noise with which they hope to scare small birds, mice, and rabbits into exposing them selves to view. They can swoop from the sky with such silent speed that their victims scarcely have time to hide. Henry feared the hawks very much, but he was too smart to fall for that screeching noise. Instead of exposing himself, Henry would press his little body motionless as close to the surface of whatever he happened to be perched upon and remained in that posistion until danger passed away.

When Henry was not busy gathering food for himself and Jenny, he would perch upon a limb and sing songs in a loud voice in hopes of attracting attention of larger birds to himself, rather than allow them to search for Jenny. His plan was to lure larger birds into chasing him and to leave Jenny's nest undiscovered. If larger birds did try to attack Henry, he would flit in and about trees and shrubs having closely matted leaves making it almost impossible for the larger more clumbsy birds to play tag with him. At those times, he would wait for them to almost catch him, but he would skillfully dodge them and then lead them on a merry chase farther away from Jenny's nest.

One morning Granny heard Henry creating a terrible noise. She had been sweeping her kitchen. She carried her broom with her to the back porch just in time to see a huge black crow perched upon the banister not more than three feet from Jenny's nest! He was moving toward it while Henry was using his wings to flail the crow with all his might, but the crow just ignored him. The crow was intent upon raiding Jenny's nest. Granny burst through the open doorway and shouted "shoo!" as she took a whack at the crow with her broom. The startled crow flew a lumbering course into the forest with Henry in hot pursuit. Granny peered into the nest to see if Jenny was alright. She was thankful that Jenny was unharmed.

A few days later, Granny saw both Henry and Jenny flitting in and out of the nest. They returned from trips into the forest every few minutes carrying small moths with their beaks. They staggered their trips in such a manner that their nest was never left unguarded. Sure enough, what Granny has suspected was true. She looked inside the nest and saw four little balls of fuzz, with bright yellow beaks almost as large as their tiny bodies. Their beaks were held wide open as they began chirping and begging for food. Granny was an excellent cook, but she knew that only Henry and Jenny knew what to feed their babies. Granny knew that the babies would be well fed.

Granny was really proud of her new neighbors. She would treat her two grand daughters and her friends to a look at the Wren Babies whenever they came to visit. It does not take many days for baby birds to grow feathers and to learn how to fly. One morning when Granny went to sweep her porch, she did not see either Henry or Jenny anywhere. She also did not hear the contented little noise "Zee zee zee zee" that they made when they were feeding their babies. A twinge of sadness filled Granny's heart as she parted the flower and looked inside. Just as she suspected, Henry and Jenny's babies had flown away. Only the cute little nest remained along with a lovely memory.

Granny rested the bottom of her broom upon the porch floor, folded her hands one on top of the other upon the top of the brook stick, and rested her chin upon her hands. While daydreaming, she gazed into the blue sky above the dark green forest, looking at nothing in particular as she contemplated the mysteries of life. She was deep in thought about the Seasons of winter and spring, the passing of summer and the coming of fall. She thought of love and birth, of life, renewal, and change.

Her mind gradually returned to the awareness of the sweet fragrant scent of her flowers as it wafted upon the breeze which was also moving a whisp of her hair across her face. As her daydream was ending and reality returned to her mind, hark! What was that distant sound which she could faintly hear coming from deep inside the forest? It was the call of a wren! Could that be Jenny or Henry? Or could it be the first notes of music which the World had ever heard coming from the throat of one of their babies? Granny smiled as she returned inside her house. She could not help but wonder if Jenny and Henry would return to her flower-pots again next year.

James E. Martin

THE DUCKBILLED PLATYPUS

THE DUCKBILLED PLATYPUS

A duckbilled platypus is an animal furry and fat
Does not look like a dog, does not look like a cat
No other critter on earth comes close to looking like that
It is half animal and the other part bird
And lays eggs like a duck, I'll bet that you have never
heard
Does it know how to howl, or does it simply quack?
Does it sleep on its tummy or lay on its back?
It has a flat beak like a duck, front feet like a goose
But its back feet have claws on toes that are separate
and loose
You should not bother looking for ears
Its head looks like a duck's, but no ears appears
Ducks have cute little tails turned up like the brim of
a hat,
But a platypus has a tail like a beaver's that is chubby
and flat
It can live on land or in water that is deep,
Can swim like an otter or run on its feet
It can be choosy when it comes time to eat
Be it bugs on the land or fish from the deep
It is a cute little fellow with fur that is brown
That is fuzzy, fine, and as soft as down
Unlike a bird, it has no wings,
It cannot fly, and it cannot sing
But it does not care, because it is too busy being what it
is, one of a kind,
Lives near the bottom of the world, but does not mind
Australia is where it takes its place
To make its home, to show its face
You may never have chance to visit its home,
For that is a very long way to roam,
But the next time you visit a zoo
Ask to see a platypus or two.
I'll bet that you will want to take it home with you.

James E. Martin

With country love,
Grandpa Ed.

Written for and presented to Mrs. Polk's 1995 second grade class, White Sulphur Springs Elementary School, West Virginia

GRANDPA ED'S BEDTIME STORIES

THE MYSTERY OF
THE MISSING EGG

BY JAMES E. MARTIN

James E. Martin

THE MYSTERY OF THE MISSING EGG

A large speckled hen lived on a farm. She always laid big brown eggs. She was a happy hen who walked contentedly about the barnyard with her friends, clucking and scratching in the loose dirt. She was very proud of her big brown eggs. Each day when she lay one, she would cackle with joy. She cackled so loudly that she could be heard at the far corners of the barnyard. The farmer was pleased to have such a handsome hen on his farm.

Then one day shortly before Easter, something very unusual happened. Speckled Hen was resting in her nest one afternoon just as she always did after a busy morning of bug catching, clucking, and ground scratching. Now is was time for her to lay her daily egg. She placed it in the center of her soft nest as always. She began cackling just as she slways did when she stopped short and became spellbound. When she looked at her new egg, it did not look like any egg that she had ever laid before. It was a beautiful jewel. Instead of being plain brown, it was an egg of many colors. She could not believe her eyes. After she overcame her shock, she invited the other barnyard hens to look at her wonderful egg. The cackling and excitement became so loud, the farmer's wife came to see if a fox had gotten into the hen house. She always carried a basket into which she collected the eggs each day. When she came to Speckled Hen's nest, she, too, could not believe her eyes! Instead of the usual brown egg she always found there, there was the beautiful multi-colored egg in the nest. She thought it was a miracle.

She ran to the farmhouse in great excitement. She called her husband and Ray and Faye, her little twins, to see the wonderful egg that Speckled Hen had laid.

"What kind of an egg is it?" asked the farmer.

"We know, We know, Daddy," both of the twins shouted at the same time. "It's an Easter egg!"

Both parents agreed that must be true. They were so excited that they called many of their friends to tell them the news. The word soon spread throughout the community, so, before long, crowds of people from miles around came to see the wonderful egg, including the proud hen who laid t.

Not to be one to avoid attracting attention to himself, the town's mayor announced that he was declaring the Saturday before Easter as 'Speckled Hen Day.' He instructed the community women and the children to color Easter eggs by the hundreds. He also instructed the men of the fire department to spend early Saturday morning hiding the eggs on the hillside behing the village park. He ordered the school's band leader to provide music for a big parade to start at noon Saturday, after he made a speech, ofcourse.

The special day arrived and the fire department hid the eggs, including the mystery egg, for the children to find. The village square filled with a large crowd who had come to see the celebration. The mayor was joined upon a flag-draped platform by the Speckled Hen, the farmer, the farmer's wife, and the twins, Ray and Faye. It was a fine day for a parade and an Easter egg hunt. As mayors so often do, this one launched into a long-winded speech about the glorious speckled hen, the wonderful egg, how it was going to make the village of Hay Seed, USA famous, and on and on. Everyone was becoming nervous. The majorettes were wanting to prance, the band wanted to toot horns and beat drums, the horses were becoming restless, the paint of the faces of the clowns was melting and starting to run, and the rotund Mrs. Falsetto was perspiring as she waited to sing The National Anthem.

The mayor finally ran out of hot air, so the parade began.

The mayor had announced that the lucky child who would find the mystery egg would get to join him on the platform after the egg hunt was over. That child would get to have its picture taken with the mayor and would be given a twenty five dollar savings bond. The highschool coach blew the starting whistle and the egg hunt began. Hundreds of children scampered over the park finding eggs everywhere they turned. The egg hunt was a great success. The children were happy. When no more eggs could be found, the egg hunt was declared over. It was the plan that the child who found the mystery egg would come forward and hand it to the mayor. The crowd waited and waited, but nobody came forward with the mystery egg. An uneasy murmur passed through the crowd then they grew silent. Parents searched through their children's egg baskets, but the mystery egg was nowhere to be seen. Something very strange had happened.

The mayor was very red faced and flustered. He was feeling sort of silly. Being a politician, he could not stand even the slightest criticism

He was sweating and squirming. He was also becoming irritated when people asked, "What are you going to do, Mr. Mayor?" they asked.

"This calls for an investigation!" he stormed.

The mayor snapped at his driver, "Go get Sam Snoop, the village detective. Tell him to come here at once."

In a short while, Sam Snoop arrived wearing a 'super fly' hat and a white trench coat, in spite of the hot weather. He was carrying a magnifying glass in one hand and a clip board in the other. He was also accompanied by his young blood hound pup, McSniff, Crime Dog In Training. Detective Snoop cast his gaze above the crowd as though he was all seeing, all knowing. He acted as though he was sniffing the air. He entered the park with long sweeping strides followed by the mayor and a cluster of people. He realized that this was a problem which he could not solve, but also being a politician, he could not let it be known that he did not have a clue.

With McSniff and his sensitive nose, the situation was a different matter. On his own and unnoticed, he began to sniff about. Earlier and also unnoticed and out of sight, Pesky Gopher had been busy digging a new tunnel through the soft dirt along the fence on the back edge of the park. Pesky had no idea what was taking place up on top of the ground. He especially had no idea that an Easter egg hunt was taking place. He was doing what gophers dearly love to do. He was digging in the dirt. Well, wouldn't you just know, Pesky dug his tunnel right under the very spot where the Mystery Egg was hidden. Unknown to him as he passed through, the Mystery Egg fell into the tunnel behind him.

I'm almost sure that you have already figured out ahead of me what was about to happen next. That's right. McSniff went sniffing along that fence row and found Pesky Gopher's hole. Now, had he been a big dog, he would not have done what he was about to do next, but because he was only a small pup, he slipped his body right down into that tunnel and became the hero of the day when he reappeared carrying the Mystery Egg in his mouth!

Everybody was happy. The mayor puffed and beamed all over. Speckled Hen was happy once more and could quit crying. The crowd was pleased with the good time had by all. McSniff was awarded the savings bond which was to be applied to his later expences when he attended the Detective Dog Training Academy. The farmer and his wife took Speckled Hen home and placed the Mystery Egg in her nest where she could admire it every day. She became highly respected by the other

153

James E. Martin

creatures who lived on or near the farm as a 'hen about town.' She often had afternoon visits by Mrs. Goose, Mrs. Turkey, Mrs. Marsh Hare, Mrs. Field Mouse, and, ofcourse, Detective Dog McSniff who provided security for the Mystery Egg.

GRANDPA ED'S BEDTIME STORIES

JODAPHUR

JAMES E. MARTIN

James E. Martin

JODAPHUR

Once there was a baby donkey named Jodaphur. He lived with his mother, Jenny and father, Jack on a large farm where dozens of swift race horses also lived. The wealthy people who owned the farm went ga ga over expensive race horses. The horses slept inside the most modern stables, were attended day and night by stablemen who bathed them daily and brushed their hair. Their manes and tails were kept trimmed and their feet and shoes were examined every day. If the horses went out of doors during bad weather, their bodies were covered by waterproof blankets. Doctors were called to the stable if a horse had the slightest sniffle. The feed and hay which they ate was the finest that money could buy. Even the clean straw upon which they slept was better than ordinary horses had to eat. Their beds were replaced with fresh straw every day. From the first light until after darkness the Owner, the stablemen, the trainers, and jockeys, who dressed in fancy brightly colored silk racing suits, tended to the racing horses' every need.

Jack and Jenny, on the other hand, were given no respect at all. No one ever brushed their long fuzzy hair or gave them a bath. They were not given fancy food to eat and they shared a drafty old box stall in an open sided equipment shed hidden from the fine stables where the race horses lived.

Little Jodaphur seldom saw his parents during daylight hours, because both Jack and Jenny worked hard from daybreak until dark pulling heavily loaded donkey carts seven days every week. They spent part of each day pulling the donkey carts through the stables where the soiled bedding from the race horse stalls would be piled high upon their loads until nothing more would stay in place. The ill tempered stablemen never had a kind word to say to the lowly donkeys. They were called unkind names such as "dumb mule" or "stubborn brute." Many times, rather than commanding the donkeys to move forward, they were painfully prodded into motion with a pitchfork, or were whopped upon their backsides with a scoop shovel. Once the race horse stalls were cleaned, and the waste was hauled to the dung heap, the donkeys were used to haul hay, grain, and fresh straw from the barns to the stables for the race horses to use. In addition to that, Jack and Jenny hauled heavy loads of wood chips and sawdust to be used in the walkways down the center of the long stables.

156

When Jadaphur was born, the news flashed throughout the stables and the farm house. His arrival caused almost as much excitement as the birth of a racehorse colt. Maybe the excitement was because Jadaphur was so tiny, but it must have also been because he was so cute. He was a sight to see! At first, he was only about two feet tall. He looked very much like a stuffed toy. He had long ears just like his parents. Most of his body was a light tan, but his face and belly were as white as snow. He had two large brown eyes and a stubby little tail. From his earliest days, he loved to run in a rocking hobby horse manner often kicking his back feet higher than his head just for fun.

The wealthy owner of the farm had two tiny grand-daughters who also lived with him at the farm house. They became so excited when told about Jodaphur's birth, they could hardly wait to see him. It was truly love at first sight. A visit with Jodaphur became an almost daily event. The little girls played with him, helped feed him, brought him lumps of sugar, and brushed his downy hair.

Donkeys do not grow to become very large animals, so Jadaphur grew very slowly and remained little for a long time. The little girls were pleased about that. It meant that they could have good times with their cuddly little friend for a much longer time than they could have if he grew really big. As Jodaphur did grow a bit larger, he also grew stronger. When he was a year old, the little girls had a birthday party for him. Grandfather surprised then with a gift for Jadaphur. He had hired a man to build the little donkey a brightly painted donkey cart with a driver seat just wide enough to seat the little girls side by side. He also hired a harness maker to make Jodaphur a little black leather harness decorated with silver rings and buckles.

Grandfather fitted the harness upon little Jadaphur and the donkey cart was hitched to the harness. The little girls took turns leading Jodaphur around in circles inside the shed. They squealed with delight. Jodaphur also seemed to enjoy this new game with his little friends. Grandfather reminded the little girls that Jodaphur was still very small and was not very strong.

Although he had the cart made large enough for both of them to ride at the same time, they would need to only give Jadaphur light loads to pull as his strength increased over time. He promised that both could ride upon the seat when the time was right.

The little girls never grew tired of playing with Jodaphur. He became so accustomed to pulling the donkey cart that it seemed very natural to him. But, as Jodaphur grew, he also began to get just a wee bit naughty. Sometimes the little girls did not realize that Jodaphur could become tired after working so hard. One day, he decided that he had had enough, so he did something that donkeys the world over have done since the beginning of time – He just sat down and refused to budge! Try as they might, they could not get Jodaphur to move. He even refused to eat sugar cubes, his favorite food. He was just showing a little stubborn streak, just like little girls sometimes do when they toot their lower lips out and pout. They finally tied Jodaphur's halter strap to a post so that he could not run away and injure himself, then went in search of their grandfather. When they told him what Jodaphur had done, he laughed very loud and told the little girls to leave the donkey alone; that he will get up on his feet when he gets ready.

One night, a terrible storm happened. The rain poured for hours without stopping. Strong gusts of wind caused everything not tied down to fly through the air. The noise made by the wind was terrible to hear, but the most scary of all was the booming thunder and the dreadful streaks of lightning. The entire storm seemed to be right down at ground level. At times the lightning was so bright that it lit the sullen night as though it were mid day.

No one could sleep because of the noise. Inside the stables, the high spirited racehorses were in panic. The electricity had been knocked out and the night watchmen were talking on the telephone to grandfather inside the farmhouse on the hill. They urged him to call the day-crew stable hands back to work to help quiet the horses, lest they injure themselves. When they arrived, they were kept busy trying to calm the frightened horses. The horses pranced and trembled with every crash of thunder. The brilliant flashes of lightning caused them to go wild. In order to see, the stablemen had to use flashlights. The ghostly sight of the flashlight beams dashing about in the periods of inky darkness caused the horses to panic even more. The stable workers were in great danger of being trampled by the powerful horses when the men entered the stalls to attach blindfolds over the horses' eyes so that they could no longer see the lightning. With a blindfold in place, a horse would began to grow calm. Their fears were further calmed when the men installed padded ear muffs over the horses' ears.

The storm raged on throughout the night and all of the next day without stopping. Water was dripping everywhere, with the soggy ground turning into mud with every step. The stable workers exercised the race

158

horses inside a roofed pavilion normally used for horse shows, since the weather outside was not fit for man nor beast. Meanwhile, over at the donkey stable, life went on as usual. Jack and Jenny were hitched to the donkey carts just as they were on any other day. No thought was given as to how wet and cold they may become in the pouring rain. Their handlers wore rain coats, rain hats, and rubber boots when they went out of doors. The race horse feed, hay, and steraw was carefully shielded from the rain by waterproof sheets, but the donkeys received no protection at all. It was work as usual for them.

Jodaphur had not been forgotten by his sweet little friends. Just as the stable workers, the girls arrived at his stable wearing high rubber boots and bright yellow raincoats complete with hoods covering their heads. They looked like oversized yellow mushrooms! They came to take care of their little friend, to be sure that he was fed, safe, and dry. They brought a blanket kept dry inside a plastic trash bag to cover him. They hugged him tightly and calmed his fear. They also brought him some oats and sugar cubes to eat. After they brushed his hair and talked to him, he eventually lay upon a bed of straw and went to sleep. The girls lay and cuddled close against their fuzzy little friend, pulled a warm blanket over both him and themselves where all three slept the remainder of the night.

The storm did not end with the arrival of daylight. The thunder and lightning had stopped, but the rain kept pouring for days. The worst fears were beginning to spread, because there was so much water, there was no place for it to go. At first, small ponds appeared in low spots, then they spread out to join other ponds which created larger ponds. The large ponds expanded to join others to form lakes. Soon the rivers overflowed their banks so that only hilltops were visible above the water.

The girls' grandfather forsaw the emergency coming. While he still had time to react, he made an arrangement with another stable owner no longer in business who lived a hundred miles away in the mountains. He agreed to provide stable space for Grandfather's prized horses for as long as necessary during and after the storm. While the highways were still open, Grandfather hired truck drivers to move his horses to safety.

"Please Grandfather! Please! Don't allow little Jodaphur and his parents to drown," pleaded the little girls. "They won't take up much room, and just think how hard Jack and Jenny have worked for you."

Grandfather said, "I am so proud of you for thinking of poor helpless animals. I will send Jack and Jenny along with the others, but we will keep Jodaphur here on the high ground where our house stands. He can share the garage with our dog and cats. He will be safe right here with you."

"Alright!" shouted the little girls as they hugged their grandfather.

It was not long before they were hugging Jodaphur, too. The girls made him a bed of straw in one corner of the garage. They were amused when the dog and cats also made their bed upon the straw with Jodaphur. It was no fun watching the rain through the windows, so the girls had fun with Jodaphur taking they, the dog, cats, and their dolls for rides on the donkey cart inside the garage.

Having their pets to play with kept the girls from seeing the great worry the adults were having. The rain kept failing as though it would never stop. Only tree tops were visible above the fields and houses. Only the bright red rooftops of Grandfather's stables could be seen. The machine shed where Jodaphur lived could not be seen at all. Hill tops looking like islands were covered by thousands of animals. Many families also moved their belongings to the hill tops to prevent them from washing away. Grandfather and his men also moved the farm machinery and the horse food supply to the high ground surrounding his house.

The rain stopped after six days and nights, but three weeks passed before most of the water returned inside the river channels. Another month passed before the stables and other buildings were cleared of mud and were sanitary enough to bring the horses back home. Little Jodaphur was once more living in the machine shed with his mother and father.

The flood had brought great sadness to hundreds of farm families, villagers, and town's folk for many miles of countryside. The weary people were thankful that their families were safely back home and that their lives were slowly returning to normal. They wanted some way to share their joy with all who had suffered, but had lived beyond all of the hard times. So the people agreed to have a huge Fourth of July parade and picnic on the city streets. Everybody who wished could enter the parade, even if it was only families holding hands and marching to show their joy.

The little girls' grandfather was so pleased that he was able to save his valuable horses, he entered a few of the older gentler ones in the parade. The stable workers decorated the horses' manes and tails with many brightly colored ribbons. The horses' bodies were bathed and brushed until they glistened in the sunlight. Each one wore shin wraps from their ankles up to their knees on all four legs making it look as though they were wearing snow white stockings. Each horse's bridle contained silver rings and buckles and each rider wore brightly colored silk racing costumes. The crowd oohed and aahed as the beautiful horces pranced by, but what they saw next following the horses caused the people to lift their voices in a thunderous cheer.

Down the middle of the street came little Jodaphur wearing his black leather harness trimmed with silver rings and buckles pulling his brightly painted donkey cart! His four little hooves were polished a glossy black and he wore a big red ribbon in his mane. He looked so cute, but what was more, riding side by side on the seat of the cart, wearing sun bonnets and flowered cotton print dresses, were the two little sisters. Each was holding one of the family's fat cats upon her lap. The family dog, tied to the cart by a long leash, quietly trotted alongside the donkey cart. Jodaphur and his friends seemed to know that they were very lucky to be alive that wonderful day.

GRANDPA ED'S CHILDREN STORIES

PEDRO PELICAN

JAMES E. MARTIN

PEDRO THE PELICAN

The first time I saw Pedro Pelican, he was perched atop a warf post at the port of New Orleans. He wasn't doing anything in particular and neither was I. It was easy for me to see that he was doing less in particular than I was. At least, I appeared to be awake, but he appeared to be sound asleep. I assume that he was asleep, because he looked as though he was asleep. Besides, he didn't open his eyes when I clapped my hands loudly to attract his attention, and, furthermore, he didn't open his eyes when a fat squat tugboat chugged past within yards of his location. The tug's pilot blew a loud warning blast on the boat's whistle, but Pedro didn't as much as quiver a feather. The wake caused by that boat was so high that I had to back off a few steps, when the water struck the base of the pier with such force that it broke above it sending spray several yards across the deck. Pedro did not even notice.

I had never seen a pelican before, so since he was allowing me such an undisturbed close-up view, this is as good a time to describe him as I will ever get. Perhaps you have never seen a pelican, either.

Well, he was about four feet long from the tip of his beak to the tip of his stubby tail. He beak, alone, was as long as his neck, and his neck was almost as long as his body. His head and neck were covered by short fuzzy white down. His body from the base of his long neck to his tail was covered by short brown feathers flecked by streaks of grey. He had bright pinkish red legs with huge webbed feet. As he sat there sleeping atop his large feet, he appeared to avoid falling from his perch by leaning back upon the tip of his stumpy tail. Just like myself, I know that he could not avoid how he looked, but, to me, he looked very comical sitting there with his neck arched back toward his body and his very long beak tucked tightly against his chest.

My amusement increased to laughing out loud when Pedro was rudely awakened and almost knocked off his perch when another equally large pelican also tried to land atop the narrow post where Pedro was sleeping. At last I could see that Pedro had a wing span of at least six feet as he struggled to keep his footing atop that post. His powerful flapping allowed him to keep the spot, having driven the intruder away. Now I would see his beady little eyes for the first time. Pedro was truly a comical bird..

163

James E. Martin

Now that he was awake, he also saw me for the first time. I don't know if he thought that I was comical looking too but he didn't show any special interest in me as he stared straight ahead with his beak still tucked tightly against his chest. He also took a couple of quick wags of his tail as though he was testing to see if it was still there and if it was still working following the collision.

Without showing his intentions, Pedro suddenly dove off the post head first appearing in danger of crashing into the water when, just in time, he spread his wings and glided effortlessly toward the open sea with the tips of his wings sometimes touching the water. It was becoming late evening as he passed out of sight. My meal time had arrived, so I returned to my ship.

The next time I saw Pedro, was on the Pacific Ocean exit to the Panama Canal next to the great port city of Balboa. My ship had docked and I was taking a late afternoon stroll along the banks of the canal watching an endless convoy of ships exiting and fading from view as they nosed out to sea. Once more, Pedro was sitting atop a warf post sound asleep. He must have been taking his afternoon nap. I thought to myself, "This fellow certainly does get around."

Almost as if an alarm went off in his head, Pedro came fully awake. He snapped his large beak to one side just in time to see a flight of seven other pelicans gliding silently by in a close head to tail straight line formation just like a flight of military jets. The birds flew so close to each other, they seemed to be strung together like a strand of beads. Just as they were passing Pedro's location, he lifted himself off the warf post with several powerful flaps of his wings and silently joined the others at the end of the line.

I watched that funny sight of what looked like a game of follow the leader. Whatever the lead pelican did, the others would imitate exactly. It was what I heard other military men jokingly refer to as the 'Panamanian Airforce!' If the lead pelican would make a dip in flight and then return to the original altitude, every other pelican in the line would dip at almost the exact spot and also regain altitude. If the leader flapped his wings three times to maintain flight speed, all of the others did likewise. If he banked to the right, the others banked to the right. If he banked to the left, they banked to the left, but each move was end to end just like the wagging motion of the tail of a kite.

Suddenly, I saw the leader fold his wings to his sides and plunge headfirst approximately fifty feet straight downward into the canal. Guess what, seven other pelicans (including Pedro) plunged headfirst into the water! Only the leader went out of sight beneath the water. The others just plopped down and bobbed about on the surface as though they were asking "What in the world happened?" After a minute or so, the leader resurfaced at a point several yards distance from the others, chomping his huge beak upon a fish which he had caught. Once more, without notice, the leader launched swiftly into the air, and as before, all of the others followed his every more in a close head to tail, string of beads fashion.

I learned later that pelicans have a large loose skin pouch on the front side of their necks just below their beaks where they can store partially swallowed fish for eating when they please. I had always thought that Pedro was comical looking when he flew past, but he looked as though he was down right deformed when he flew with his pouch bulging with fish!

My introduction into Pedro's world came at a time in my life when I was traveling either by ship or by flying boat to several distant places around the World over a period of almost four years. I had to remain at some very lonely locations for several weeks and sometimes for several months. It seemed to me that Pedro was always there before I arrived. He never made a sound, except when he plopped into water with a big splash. It also seemed that he never looked at me. If he did, he never let me know. He could go soaring by and act as though he was the only creature on earth. There were many times when he would pass almost at arm length as I stood upon high cliffs overlooking the ocean. I could wave my arms, clap my hands, whistle, shout – nothing attracted his attention, except fish. He seemed to have total concentration upon where he was going. Although he glided rather swiftly and without visible effort, he never seemed to be in a hurry. Once in a great while, he would flap his wings a few times to maintain altitude, but would resume gliding upon the air currents.

Many times, I have seen Pedro fold his wings into his sides and plunge into the ocean like a bomb from heights of almost one hundred feet in search of something which I could not see. After what often seemed like several minutes, long after I never expected to see him again, he would reappear a long way from where he entered the water clutching a wiggly fish in his beak. Most of the time, he would point his beak toward the sky and expertly plop the fish into his pouch. He would seem so pleased with himself and would spend a few minutes bobbing in the water like a cork.

It was mid-morning one bright sunlit day when I was fishing from a shoreline cliff on one of the Galapagoes Islands in the Pacific Ocean.

165

Along with a sea minnow which I was using for bait, I fastened a small patch of white cloth to my hook just to attract the attention of fish when the bait reached the water. Some of my friends had taught me to do that when deepsea fishing from a boat. It really brought satisfactory results at those times.

On that morning, I was alone and was feeling so totally content. At least, I thought that I was alone. Just as I cast my bait high above the water, and just as it was about to reach the dark blue Pacific Ocean water, Pedro came silently soaring from behind my right side. With the speed of light, he made a mighty dive catching my bait and carrying it out of sight with him beneath the surface. Poor Pedro realized his mistake, but too late as he resurfaced from the water and began a terrorized flopping climb back into the air! My only hope of saving him was to carefully reel him in to where I was standing. My fear was that he would surely cut his throat, if he had swallowed the sharp hook.

In his state of wild panic, he did not surrender easily. It was no easy task reeling him in against the strength of his powerful wings. It was a lengthy struggle, but at last I was facing Pedro Pelican at arm's length. He was really frightened and in considerable pain not knowing what to expect next. I realized that I could get some dangerous slices upon my hands and arms if I were not very cautious of the hooks sharp point, should it be sticking through the outside skin of that huge flopping bird. For that reason, I placed my heavy fishing rod under my feet and firmly stood upon it, after which I grasped the fishing line with my left hand, and pulled Pedro toward me once more until I could clamp my right hand upon the back of his head. With that done, I moved by feet so that I could straddle his back and force him to the ground. That having been done, Pedro calmed himself and allowed me to open his beak using both hands. It was fortunate that Pedro had not swallowed my hook, but instead, it had pierced the tip end of his lower beak where it caused very little damage. I was glad that his mighty strength had not torn a chunk out of his beak which might have caused him to die. The small hole was no threat to Pedro's life, besides he would be exposed daily to the healing powers of the ocean's salty water. Pedro was certain to live a long care-free life.

I used the opportunity to pet Pedro for a while before releasing him. I marveled at his great ugliness while he must have been thinking, "They sure do grow some homely looking ole farm-boys up there in West Virginia." No matter what our first impressions of each other were, we discovered that we both were kind and gentle creatures. I, for one, wa glad that we had finally met face to face for a brief moment, and that I had the chance to touch him.

Your old country friend,
Grandpa Ed

GRANDPA ED'S BEDTIME STORIES

SPLASH PUDDLE JUMPER

SPLASH PUDDLE JUMPER

Can you remember how much fun it was to jump into a rain puddle? You would make the mud go kersplat and the water would splash. Your Mommy did not think it was so much fun; neither did anyone standing nearby who became splattered by mud. Grandpa Ed remembers when he was a little boy. He would go out of his way to wade through every mud puddle along the way to and from school. Have you done that too?

This story is about such a little boy who loved to jump into mud puddles so much and so often that his family and friends began calling him Splash Puddle Jumper. Just as people become known by their nicknames, that little boy was called Splash for his entire life. It made no difference to him if he was dressed in his play clothes or his Sunday best suit. If he saw a mud puddle, he would jump into it with both feet and make the water fly.

Splash was a good little boy who tried to be friendly and polite. He was also very good to his Mother and Father. He even got along well with his sister who was four years older than he was. His teachers and friends at school adored him. He had one fault which caused him to get into trouble sometimes. There were times when that fault caused his friends to become just a little bit angry with him. That fault was that Splash could not resist jumping into mud puddles where ever they happened to be or who ever may be near enough to get splattered. Most people just laughed about it and passed it off as a childish prank. Most adults would say, "He will get over that."

There were two people in the community, however, who did not think that Splash's prank was very funny. The first was a little girl who was Splash's age named Sadie Harper. Just like most little girls, Sadie enjoyed wearing pretty bright colored dresses, neat shiny shoes, white stockings, and lots of ribbons and bows. She thought that Splash was a dreadful naughty boy who was always trying to splash mud onto her pretty clothing.

She would scold, "Splash Starcher, I hate you!"

The other person who did not like Splash was Mr. Script, the publishers of the town newspaper. Mr. Script was a grouchy old man who never became a father. It was no surprise that Mr. Script did not like Splash, because he did not like anyone. Mr. Script did not have any friends that anyone knew of, mostly because he never did write anything nice about anyone in his newspaper. He did not like Splash because one time during a heavy rainstorm, Splash jumped into a mud puddle right in front of Mr. Script's newspaper office and splashed mud on the old man's plate glass window. From that day onward, Mr. Script would shake his head from side to side each time he saw Splash walk by.,

Mr. Script would say, "That boy will never amount to a hill of beans."

As the years passed by, Splash became a handsome youth. He was a star player on the high school basketball team. In addition to that, his class mates elected him to be Class President each of his high school years. He had many friends among students and also among adults. Sadie Harper and Mr. Script remained two people who would never find anything good to say about Splash. Of course, Splash no longer jumped into mud puddles, but his love for water was stronger than ever. He became a very strong swimmer. Splash enjoyed other sports, but his greatest love was swimming. He won many trophies on the high school swimming team and never missed an opportunity to go swimming.

Splash was a skilled student who always earned high grades in school. His closest rival was Sadie Harper. Her dislike for Splash seemed to grow stronger each year. Her grudge against Splash drove her to try to out-perform him, but try as she might, she always had slightly lower grades. She allowed that to make her even more bitter toward Splash. The night for high school graduation finally came. It is customary for the student having the highest average grades to be given the honor of addressing the graduating class as the Valedictorian; the second highest is called the Salutatorian. Splash earned the highest honor and, once more, Sadie came in second.

The high school auditorium was filled with families, neighbors, and friends as the graduation ceremonies were ready to begin. The house lights were dimmed as the high school band played the school marching song. The graduating class marched upon the stage in single file wearing their beautiful gold colored robes trimmed in white. They looked so splendid as they passed beneath the bright lights of the stage where they took seats facing the audience. The guest speaker was introduced and he made a speech about the importance of honesty, truthfulness, and good citizenship. When he finished speaking, it was time for Sadie to make her speech. She rose from her seat and made a very fine speech for which she was given a standing ovation.

It was now time for Splash to make his speech, but when his name was announced, Splash was nowhere to be seen. A buzz of confusion passed through the crowd. Everybody became greatly disturbed. Just as the school principal was beginning to announce that the Valedictorian speech would not be presented, Splash dashed upon the stage. He was covered by mud and his clothing were torn and soaked by water. His face and arms were scratched and bleeding. A pool of water began to form around his feet where it dripped from his clothing. His poor family was in shock as he calmly took his place behind the speaker's stand and delivered his speech. A very inspiring speech it was for which the crowd gave him thunderous cheers. As he took his seat beside Sadie Harper, she moved as far away from him as she could to avoid soiling her gown with mud.

She hissed at him, "Well Splash, I see that you are back to your old tricks!"

The Principal was struggling to bring calm back to the graduation ceremonies when one of the teachers gestured for him to come to the dark edge of the stage where she whispered something into his ear.

The Principal returned to the speaker's stand and said, "Friends, I have a very special announcement to make. I have just been told that we have a real live hero with us on this stage tonight. I have just learned the reason that Splash Starcher was late and then arrived soaking wet was because there was an accident on the highway leading to this school. A car carrying a lady and her two year old son was forced off the bridge into the river by a drunken driver. Splash saw the accident and, without hesitation, dived into the river and rescued the woman and her son before the rescue squad had time to arrive. I must say that this is the happiest, most outstanding graduation that I have ever attended. Splash, we are so very very proud of you."

Pleasant dreams little ones,
"Grandpa Ed"

THE ACORN AND THE RIVER

BY JAMES E. MARTIN

THE ACORN AND THE RIVER

Once there was an oak tree growing on the steep side of a high mountain ravine in West Virginia. One day an acorn fell from the tree during a thunder storm. The acorn was rolled and swept down the mountainside by a little rivulet of water created by the heavy downpour of rain. The rivulet grew larger and the acorn was carried faster and farther from the tree. Soon the rivulet reached a babbling brook.

"Where are you going Babbling Brook?" asked Rivulet.

"I am on my way to meet the creek," answered Babbling Brook, "Where are you and Acorn going?"

"We are on our way to see the Ocean," replied Rivulet.

"Well, why don't you just come along with me and we will go to the Ocean together," invited Babbling Brook.

"We would like that very much," said Acorn and Rivulet at the same time.

After being carried along for a few miles, Babbling Brook came to Country Creek. Country was having quite a tussle trying to keep all of its water inside its banks.

"Breathlessly, Country Creek asked, "Where are you going, Babbling Brook?"

"Acorn and I are on our way to see the Ocean," answered Babbling Brook.

"Well, I'm tired of fighting to control things here and I would like to see the Ocean, too. Why don't we all travel together?" replied Country Creek.

"We would like that very much," answered Babbling Brook.

So the four friends traveled with increasing speed for several miles before arriving at the banks of Rapid River. Rapid River was having a real tussle with tree trunks and limbs bounding along at high speed over and around huge boulders and shoals. Above the deafening roar of the rushing water, Rapid River shouted:

"Where are you going, Country Creek?"

"We four friends are on our way to see the Ocean," yelled Country Creek.

"Well, I have always wanted to see the Ocean, too," replied Rapid River. "I really do need a vacation, so why don't you come along with me and we will travel together."

"That sounds like a splendid idea," said Country Creek. "We would enjoy doing that."

"Let's get started, then," said Rapid River, "but prepare yourselves for a wild, rough, and rocky ride! Mr. Ocean, here we come!"

All of the travelers dived right in and, almost at once, they were zooming along at fantastic speed. They were tossing and bounding over rapids and around huge rocks in dizzying clouds of foam and spray. "Whee!" They thrilled, bounded, and crashed mile after mile between deep mountain gorges. Hours later, they broke out of the very last gorge and spread out into the quiet water of Broad River.

"Where on earth are you crazy travelers going?" chuckled Broad River.

Taking a moment to catch their breath, the friends answered, "We are on our way to see the Ocean."

"Well, you are in luck," replied Broad River. "I am packed and was planning to start making that same trip today. How would you like to travel along with me?"

"How lucky can we get?" asked Rapid River. He answered for all of the others, "We would really enjoy doing that." So off they went floating slowly upon the gentle current of Broad River.

For the first time Acorn, Rivulet, Babbling Brook, Country Creek, and Rapid River passed towns, cities, factories, freight piers, boat docks, power plants, oil tank yards, and farms. They also met fleets of powerful tug boats pushing clusters of freight barges, swimmers, fishermen, and an occasional landing of sea planes upon the water. Speedboats zipped about now and then, some pulling water skiers behind them. Every several hours, the travers came to sets of locks where long lines of barges and their tug boats awaited passage. Acorn felt so very tiny as he bobbed along with each wave in the ever widening river hour after hour, day after day, always drifting farther from his high mountain home.

After what must have been months, Broad River arrived at the shore of Old Man River. That new river was so wide, it must have been a mile to the opposite shore.

With his great booming voice, Old Man River demanded, "Where are you and your friends going, Broad River?"

174

"My friends and I are on our way to see the Ocean," replied Broad River.

"Bully!" exclaimed Old Man River. "That is great, because you see, that is where I am going, too. Why don't you be my Guest and join me for the trip?"

"Hurrah!" shouted all of the travelers at once. "We will be happy to make the trip with you."

So the friends began the journey with Old Man River, enroute to the Ocean over a thousand miles away. Acorn had never seen so much space or so much water. Old Man River was enormous. It was not long before Acorn and his friends were separated and he found himself all alone. Although he was kind and friendly, Old Man River was much too busy to pay much attention to a tiny Acorn. There were days on end when Acorn was swept along in midstream where neither shore could be seen. There was seldom a time either day or night when Acorn was out of sight of great paddle wheeled show boats, and hundreds of loaded freight barges pushed by powerful tug boats. Old Man River was busy flowing past large cities, vast swamps, and around many sand bars.

There were times when Acorn drifted close to shore where Old Man River made a sharp bend. At those times, houses, trees, piers, and row boats could be seen. Also present at those places were ducks, geese, and long legged cranes. Acorn was in danger of being eaten by hungry birds at those times, but somehow, he escaped unnoticed.

Acorn was very lonesome now. He was separated from his friends and Old Man River was much too busy making sure that all of the river traffic had enough water to float and avoid running aground upon sand bars to talk to Acorn. It has been written that 'Old Man River don't say nuthin. He don't plant taters, he don't plant cotton, and them whut plant un am soon forgotten, but Old Man River, he jus keep a'rollin along."

Sometimes Acorn was right in the path of river barges or the paddle wheels of big show boats. At those times, Acorn was churned violently in the water. There were times, too, when Acorn was floating near large towns when he would be tossed wildly by the wake of fast speed boats.

After floating for many weeks, Acorn reached the city of New Orleans. The city is such a marvelous sight with its tall high rise skyline, massive riverside warfs, and giant warehouses. Along with showboats and barges, Acorn was tossed about like a cork by the propellers of giant ocean-going ships, harbor tug boats, ferry boats, and fishing trawlers. The busy river traffic was amazing.

All the while that poor Acorn was being tossed about he continued to float toward the ocean. It took an entire day for him to pass New Orleans, but he was still on the way to his destination. Many times he was pushed along the way by huge ships who were also on their way to the open sea.

Finally, at daybreak one misty morning, Acorn could hear the roar of the Ocean as its salty waves crashed against the breakwaters along the shoreline. For a time, it seemed that Old Man River was flowing backward as the Ocean's powerful morning tide came rushing in. But, when the tide returned to the sea near noontime, it seemed as though a giant drain had been opened, and Acorn was sucked far out to sea. Caught in the wild tempest of frothy white capped waves with no land in sight, little Acorn could not help thinking of the day when he fell from the oak tree and was carried away by Rivulet.

A violent storm moved in and lasted several days. Acorn was swept helter skelter many miles on the wildest ride of his entire trip. One day, when the hurricane flooded the Alabama shoreline, Acorn was carried far upstream on the Mobile River where he was dumpoed over a dyke near the edge of a forest. His long journey was over at last. Acorn lay where he landed upon the fertile ground. Within a few days, he sprouted roots and began to grow into a beautiful sturdy oak tree, just like the one from which he fell so long ago upon that steep mountainside in Greenbrier County, West Virginia.

With Country Love and Love of Country,

Your old friend,

Grandpa Ed.

YARD BIRD

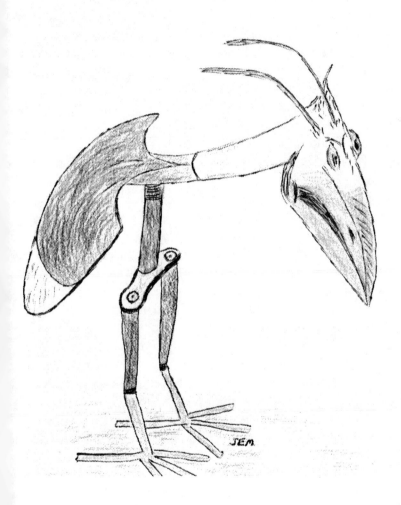

James E. Martin

YARD BIRD

One morning when Grandpa Ed walked into his lawn, he saw a large and fearsome looking bird standing near a flower bed. The bird stood motionless and was just staring at the ground. The bird was almost two feet tall with long yellow legs and a thin flat black body. He had a massive yellow beak that was long and pointed. His neck was long and curved upward. His neck, head, crest, and tail feathers were snow white. To say it mildly, that was one weird looking bird! Grandpa Ed had never seen a bird like him. He asked some of his friends if they knew what kind of a bird it was. A very old man who had traveled in many foreign countries said that he had seen a bird such as that one time in the jungles of Kooka-Monga. The natives called it a Yard Bird. This is the story that Grandpa's old friend told him.

No other bird looks like a Yard Bird. It does not have feathers, or quills, or fuzz, or plumes, or down. It is not speckled, striped, spotted, mottled, or dappled. It is not fat, plump, or boat-shaped. It is tall, skinny, and gawky looking.

A Yard Bird does not chirp, sing, squawk, crow, coo, cluck, gobble, warble, whistle, hoot, or screech. They do not hop, flop, walk, run, fly, sail, glide, dive, soar, or swim. A Yard Bird does not move at all. They just stand in one place and stare at the ground.

Yard birds do not eat seeds, worms, crumbs, fruit, fish, bugs, flies, or flowers. Actually, they never eat anything. They never open their mouths for any reason. They just stand and stare at the ground.

A Yard Bird does not lay eggs, either. Yard Birds are not ever hatched from eggs. They do not build nests, do not peck holes into trees, do not perch on limbs, live inside bird houses, or hide in grass. Actually Yard Birds do not do anything. They just stand and stare at the ground.

Yard Birds do not migrate, either. They just stand and stare at the ground.

Exactly, what does a Yard Bird look like? How will you know one if you see one? Well, he has a beak that looks somewhat like that of a pelican. He has a white top notch or crest that resembles two bent sticks. His neck is long and slender like that of a goose. His body is flat and thin like that of a sandhill crane. He is about two feet tall on legs that are long and thin like those of a heron. His yellow feet have four toes like those of a turkey.

But a Yard Bird is not related to any other bird, for you see, what Grandpa's old friend did not know, Yard Bird was created from scrap metal which Grandpa found in a junk yard. His feet are made of thin metal rods, his legs are the front wheel fork from an old bicycle, his neck and body is the metal from a round pointed shovel. His head and beak is a blade guard from a moving machine cutter bar, he eyes are bolt taps, and the crest atop his head are two pieces of bent wire.

Although Yard Bird may be ugly and cannot sing, run, build a nest, lay an egg, cannot fly, or eat worms as other birds do, he is very lovable and quite harmless. Besides, he is Grandpa's friend.

With oodles of Country Love,
Grandpa Ed.

ABOUT THE AUTHOR

James E. Martin, the son of Scottish immigrants was orphaned at the age of two. He grew to manhood on a farm owned by Foster Parents in Western Greenbrier County, West Virginia. Soon after graduating from high school, he was drafted into the World War II Army.

James spent a career with the U.S. Army spanning most of World War II, the Korean War, and part of the Viet Nam War. He career began as an artilleryman with the final thirteen years in Counter Intelligence. He was a paratrooper for twelve and one half years. After retiring, he completed an undergraduate degree at Morris Harvey College, Charleston, West Virginia.

The Author resides at Caldwell, West Virginia with Betty Jean, his Wife of fifty five years. They have two children and two granddaughters.

Throughout the past eight years, James has written many dozens of children's stories which he has read as a volunteer to five, sometimes eight, classes per week at the White Sulphur Springs, West Virginia Elementary School. The message he promoted glorifies honesty, patriotism, respect, self-reliance, and love of one's family and neighbors.

Printed in the United States
60516LVS00005B/43-153